Calculator Puzzles, Tricks and Games

by Norvin Pallas

DRAWINGS BY JOYCE BEHR

D1056483

DOVER PUBLICATIONS, INC.
NEW YORK

Published in Canada by General Publishing Company, Ltd., 30 Lesmill Road,
Don Mills, Toronto, Ontario.
Published in the United Kingdom by Constable and Company, Ltd., 3 The
Lanchesters, 162–164 Fulham Palace Road, London W6 9ER.

This Dover edition, first published in 1991, is an unabridged, unaltered republication of the work originally published by the Sterling Publishing Co., New York,
1976.

Manufactured in the United States of America
Dover Publications, Inc., 31 East 2nd Street, Mineola, N.Y. 11501

Library of Congress Cataloging-in-Publication Data

Pallas, Norvin.
    Calculator puzzles, tricks and games / by Norvin Pallas ; drawings by Joyce
Behr.
        p.   cm.
    Includes index.
    Summary: A collection of games, tricks, and puzzles which illustrate the
capabilities of a calculator.
    ISBN 0-486-26670-2 (pbk.)
    1. Calculators—Problems, exercises, etc.—Juvenile literature.
2. Mathematical recreations—Juvenile literature. [1. Calculators—
Problems, exercises, etc. 2. Mathematical recreations.] I. Behr, Joyce,
ill. II. Title.
QA75.P33   1991
510'.28—dc20
                                     90-23593
                                         CIP
                                         AC

Contents

Introduction

Now you have a new calculator.

If this is your first experience with a calculator, the chances are that you have already punched away at this and that, almost at random, just to see what would happen. But after the initial excitement wore off, hopefully, you read the directions carefully, to learn just what your instrument is capable of.

Virtually all calculators perform the four basic arithmetic functions: addition, subtraction, multiplication, and division. Let us frankly admit that as far as addition and subtraction are concerned, a home calculator is no big improvement on earlier adding machines, or even the ancient abacus. It is in multiplication, division, and more complex operations that the calculator turns into a whiz.

Even the on/off switch is of some interest, because on some instruments this will clear the machine, and on some it will not. You will have to check. Some machines will clear themselves if, after pressing the total key, you put another figure into the machine without first pressing an operations key. But a word of caution: if you are putting in a negative number, the machine will not clear, because the minus sign is an operations key.

You will want to understand clearly how to make corrections when you have hit the wrong key, which will save you many a headache and repetition. On some models depressing the add key repeatedly will cause the amount in the display to double each time, useful for some types of problems.

It is almost certain that your new calculator has a floating decimal point. If you multiply .43 by .58, your answer will be .2494, the decimal point automatically moved over to the left. But sometimes a fixed decimal point will be useful to you. If you are only interested in an answer to the nearest penny, a fixed-point decimal might give you the answer .24, or .25 if it is programmed to add on the extra penny when half or more remains. More expensive calculators will have both kinds of decimal points.

Your calculator may have a memory. Suppose you have a number in your machine, but want to put it aside temporarily while you make a different calculation. You can put it into the memory, then retrieve it again when you need it. This will save putting the figure down on paper, and later entering it into the machine again—provided you remember what you have placed in the memory.

A constant can be useful if you are doing the same type of calculation many times. Suppose you are reducing all the prices in a store by 15%. If your machine can hold the 15% as a constant, you will not have to enter it separately for each piece of merchandise. It may also be possible for you to multiply a certain amount by 15%, then the answer to that by 15%, and so on, all without placing the 15% into the machine each time.

A per cent key is something you can live without. All it does is move the decimal point two positions to the left, so that you can multiply by $67\frac{1}{2}\%$ by entering 67.5 and pressing the per cent key, instead of .675—hardly any great saving and a trivial operation for a calculator. Unless you have a great many operations of this kind, you might be better advised to handle your own decimal points. In any case, you should learn how.

Reciprocal keys, sign-changing keys, and square keys are all handy, though you can perform the same operations yourself without too much trouble. A square root key is very useful, though, because doing that yourself is a little involved.

If your instrument is equipped for scientific notation, you can enlarge the capacity of your calculator immensely. Suppose the national debt is $512,000,000,000. In scientific notation this would be written:

$$5.12 \times 10^{11}$$

All this really means is that the decimal point, which has been placed after the first significant figure, actually belongs 11 positions to the right. To transfer the above figure out of scientific notation, you would have to add 9 zeros to fill the empty positions. If the formula read:

$$5.12 \times 10^{-11}$$

this would not mean that the government had a surplus of the same amount, but only that the decimal point properly belongs 11 positions to the left.

Ordinarily, if you undertake a calculation and the decimals are too large for the machine to hold, it will simply drop off figures at the right as being insignificant. But if your calculation results in too many whole numbers, your machine will probably warn you that you have exceeded its capacity. On a scientific notation machine, however, too many whole numbers will cause the machine to jump into scientific notation. The normal windows will show the regular figure, in our case 5.12, while the two windows at the far right will show 11 or −11, as the case may be. The 10 is not shown; it is always the same.

New models are coming along all the time. Advanced machines may be programmed to calculate sines and other trigonometric functions. Models are now available which enable you to program your own machine in a small way—at this stage your calculator is turning into a computer.

This book will help you become acquainted with your calculator. Many games and stunts are offered which should be fun, and will also help you learn to work with your machine. But in the long run, your instrument is a tool, not a toy. By using it you can calculate with greater speed and accuracy— and also undertake problems that would be altogether too consuming of time and energy to solve in any other way. It will, in the end, help you to a better understanding of the world around you and how it functions.

Upside-Down Displays

Seven of the digits on a calculator, when turned upside down, will make reasonable approximations of letters of the alphabet. Solve the following problems, then read the display upside down to answer the clue. You may want to guess the answer before trying the calculation.

a. The square root of 196 and get a greeting.

b. 440 × 7 and get a musical instrument.

c. 52,043 ÷ 71 and get a snake-like fish.

- d. 30,000,000 − 2,457,433 × 2 and find out why a wife may give in to her husband.

e. $7,964^2$ + 7,652,049 and get the name of a large oil corporation.

f. 711 × 10,000 − 9,447 and get a competing oil corporation.

g. 53.5149 − 51.4414 ÷ 29 and find a farmer's storage place. (NOTE: If your calculator prints a 0 before a decimal point, divide by 2.9 instead of 29.)

h. 15^2 − 124 × 5 and get a distress signal.

i. 2 − 1.4351 ÷ 7 and get a name for a wolf. (See note on g.)

j. 159 × 357 − 19,025 and get a beautiful young lady.

k. 471 × 265 + 410,699 and learn what a snake does.

l. 99^2 − 2,087 and get a rise.

m. 1 − .930394 ÷ .9 and get a telephone greeting. (See note on g.)

n. 217 × 121 − 8,550 and get a kind of pop.

o. .161616 ÷ 4 and find out what Santa Claus said when you asked him for a new yacht. (See note on g.)

(Answers on page 76)

A Few Lines About Nines

Now that you have an electronic calculator, you don't have to worry about checking your work, right? Wrong, sad to say, since calculators can make mistakes: batteries run down, keys stick, or something goes haywire inside. And of course it is easier to blame the calculator than to admit that we hit a wrong key, or maybe attempted something the machine was not designed to handle. When checking your work, or some-one else's, you may want a quick check to avoid repetition.

The process of casting out 9's is the traditional method for checking a difficult problem. The basis for this technique is cross-adding, reducing each number in the problem to a smaller number by adding the digits together. Suppose we have the number 891562. We can add it across as follows:

$$8 + 9 + 1 + 5 + 6 + 2 = 31 = 3 + 1 = 4$$

Notice that the answer would be just the same if we left the 9 out of the problem:

$$8 + 1 + 5 + 6 + 2 = 22 = 2 + 2 = 4$$

What we have done basically is to take out all the 9's and multiples of 9 throughout the problem, and the number which remains is the equivalent of the remainder in division.

$$\frac{99062 \text{ remainder } 4}{9)891562}$$

In the problems that follow, the original problem is given at the left, with the answer often reduced to a single digit. In the proof on the right, each number in the original problem is reduced to a single digit, and then we go through the problem just as though this was the original problem.

$$
\begin{array}{ll}
3417 & 6 \\
512 & 8 \\
6481 & 1 \\
\underline{17} & \underline{8} \\
\overline{10427} = 14 = 5 & \overline{23} = 5
\end{array}
$$

$$
\begin{array}{ll}
3417 & 6 \\
\underline{-724} & \underline{4} \\
\overline{2693} = 20 = 2 & \overline{2}
\end{array}
$$

$$
\begin{array}{ll}
3417 & 6 \\
\underline{-728} & \underline{8} \\
\overline{2689} = 25 = 7 & -2 + 9 = 7
\end{array}
$$

(Note that if your subtraction yields a negative answer, you must add 9 to complete the proof.)

$$
\begin{array}{ll}
3417 & 6 \\
\underline{\times 621} & \underline{9} \\
\overline{2121957} = 27 = 9 & \overline{54} = 9
\end{array}
$$

$$
\begin{array}{ll}
3417 & 6 \\
623)\overline{2128791} & 2)\overline{3}
\end{array}
$$

Proof: $6 \times 2 = 12 = 3$

$$
\begin{array}{ll}
3400 \text{ r. } 606 & 7 \text{ r. } 3 \\
626)\overline{2129006} & 5)\overline{2}
\end{array}
$$

Proof: $7 \times 5 + 3 = 38 = 11 = 2$

$$
\begin{array}{ll}
3417 & 6 \\
\sqrt{11675889} & \sqrt{9}
\end{array}
$$

Proof: $6^2 = 36 = 9$

$$\sqrt{81676104}^{\ \ 9037\ r.\ 8735} \qquad \sqrt{6}^{\ \ 1\ r.\ 5}$$

Proof: $1^2 + 5 = 6$

These proofs will not catch all possible errors. If you copy the problem down wrong, only a miracle can give you the right answer. If you reverse digits in the answer, or misplace the decimal, the proofs will not help. And there is coincidence —perhaps one chance in nine—that your proof will come out if you make an error in more than one digit. Are the proofs still worth while? You be the judge.

Sports Figures

1. The ball is on the Cleveland Browns' 5-yard line. On the next play the Browns commit a flagrant violation of the rules, which would normally call for a 15-yard penalty. However, there is a special rule that a team may not be penalized more than half the distance to its goal. On the following play the Minnesota Vikings are penalized 15 yards. Then the Browns are penalized, then the Vikings, and so on, while the customers go out for refreshments. Where will the ball eventually land?

2. At the beginning of the baseball season, you make a bet with a friend. For every game the Mudville Nine plays, you will pay him 5¢ when they lose, and he will pay you 7¢ when they win. The season consists of 156 games. When the season is over, you find that you came out exactly even. How many games did the Mudville Nine win?

3. If Babe Ruth hit 60 home runs in 154 games, and Roger Maris hit 61 home runs in 162 games, who had the better record?

(Answers on page 76)

Hit It!

Here is an absorbing game which you can play with friends, or as a form of calculator solitaire. To begin, have each player put a random five-digit number into his calculator. He then copies this number on a scrap of paper, and exchanges this paper with another player. The object of the game is to be the first player to, *strictly by multiplying*, make the digits showing on his calculator match the number on the scrap of paper he has received. If the number to be hit is smaller than his original entry in the display, the player can lower it by multiplying by a number less than one, and vice versa. As the player approaches the point where his display matches his target, he must multiply by numbers which are closer and closer to one. The decimal places which appear when multiplying are ignored in the final result, but cannot be ignored by the player as his multiplication proceeds.

When playing against someone else, speed is the object, and it might be a good tactic to close the gap by making many swift multiplications by numbers which don't change the display a great deal. When you play by yourself, however, you can judge your success by the number of multiplications you perform, rather than the time it takes you. This puts the accent on accuracy rather than speed.

You may want to try to create certain patterns in the display rather than simply hit a random number. Why not attempt to show eight digits in consecutive order in your final display? Or perhaps a pattern, like 12312312 or 24242424, or even 22222222. You can even shoot for your birthday, expressed in eight digits. If you need a zero for the first digit, remember to enter the appropriate decimal point. This won't affect the multiplication process.

ESP

Extra-sensory perception—the ability to read minds, predict the future, sense distant happenings, influence inanimate objects, and so on—is a subject of much popular speculation, though many scientists discount it. For our purposes, let us assume that your calculator neither possesses nor transmits ESP, and that when we make it appear to do so, we are resorting to trickery.

Tricks may appear different, yet all involve essentially the same principles. There is a secret number known only to your victim. If it is a made-up number he had better write it down so he will remember it, but if it is his birthdate or age or telephone number, presumably there won't be any problem. You have him go through a series of rapid calculations on the machine, which supposedly will conceal the information, but lo! There at the end it stands revealed in the display. Another method is to have him subtract out his secret number at the end, and you will give him the number remaining in the display, even though the calculations apparently depended on a number that was unknown to you.

Let us suppose that your best friend was born May 4, 1960. It is not necessary for you to know this number in advance; it makes a better trick if you do not. Have him follow your instructions on his calculator, but do not look at the figures in the machine:

"Enter the month of your birth."	5
"Multiply by 100."	500
"Add the day of the month of your birth."	504
"Multiply by 10,000."	5040000
"Add the year of your birth."	5041960

Now ask to see the calculator, and you can easily tell him the month, day, and year of his birth. Of course this stunt is much too obvious to use, so we must add other complications to confuse the issue. But remember, in spite of all the complications, we are doing essentially just what we showed above!

Now for some possible complications. Instead of multiplying by 100, we can multiply first by 20, and then by 5, which produces the same result. Another method is to undershoot it a little: 11 × 9 + the month of your birth again. Another method is to overshoot it a little: 17 × 6 — the month of your birth and (for showmanship purposes only, since it is really essential to subtract it twice), "Oh, I didn't see you do it, subtract the month of your birth again."

To multiply by 10,000, we can use 600 × 50 ÷ 3, or any other combination that will equal the same thing. Be careful, though: we cannot add or subtract at this stage, because multiplying and dividing will affect the figure that is already in the calculator in the way we desire, but addition or subtraction will not.

For a further complication, you can add 6 after the first step, an extraneous number really having no bearing on our main problem. Remember that you can always add or subtract extraneous numbers any place in the problem—provided you are able to keep track of what is happening to them.

As a final complication, select as a "volunteer" someone whose telephone number you have looked up in advance. Suppose his telephone number is 741-8106. This is larger than 6,120,000 (later you will see where this number came from), so subtract as follows:

$$\begin{array}{r} 7418106 \\ -6120000 \\ \hline 1298106 \end{array}$$

Remember this number, or write it down. Now you are ready

to perform your stunt. Ask your carefully selected volunteer
to do the following:

"Enter the month of your birth."	5
"Add 6."	11
"Multiply by 17."	187
"Multiply by 6."	1122
"Subtract the month of your birth."	1117
"Subtract it again, and this time do it right."	1112
"Add the day of the month of your birth."	1116
"Multiply by 600."	669600
"Multiply by 50."	33480000
"Divide by 3."	11160000
"Add the year of your birth."	11161960
"Add 1,298,106" (sometimes you must subtract).	12460066

"Make the following calculation carefully:
      subtract key, the month of your birth,
      the day of your birth in two digits (if
      you were born before the 10th of the
      month, precede it with a zero), the year
      of your birth."   7418106

Ask your victim the significance of that number, and he
will be startled to admit that it is his telephone number!

To help you make up your own variations, let us see exactly
what happened. We put in your friend's complete birthdate,
and finally subtracted it out again, which in effect left the
machine cleared of those figures. But we put in an extraneous
6, so let's see what became of it. We multiplied 6×102 (17×6)
—ignore all additions and subtractions— $\times$ 10,000 (600 $\times$ 50
$\div$ 3) = 6120000. Because his telephone number was larger than
this, we added the difference.

Making Allowances

1. You have convinced Dad that you deserve a raise in your allowance and only the amount remains to be decided. You tell Dad that your wants are quite modest, and all you are asking is a penny the first day, 2¢ the second day, 4¢ the third day, and so on for a 30-day month. Dad laughs, reminding you that that is an old one, that he tried it on his own father thirty years ago. But Dad says if you can give him an exact answer to your proposition, then he will counter with a proposition of his own. Be careful now, he wants an *exact* answer, and the problem may be too large for your calculator.

2. Of course you were able to give Dad the correct answer, so now here is his proposition. He will increase your allowance by (a) $5; or (b) 1¢ for the first day, 2¢ for the second day, 3¢ for the third day, and so on for 30 days; or (c) will give you an increase of 1¢ for the first day, and 3% more every day after that through 30 days—of course he will pay you every day to the nearest correct penny. The joker is that you must make your decision without resorting to your calculator. You decide you had better take the safe $5, but you wonder if you gained or lost on the deal. When figuring (c), the complete decimal will soon be lost on your calculator, but solve it the best you can within the limitations of your calculator.

3. A friend is much impressed with your ingenuity and/or calculator, and tells you he has an allowance problem of his own. He can afford to pay a total of $50 a month to his five children, but the problem is how to divide the money among them. He thinks they should be paid according to the grade they are in in school, so that a child in the tenth grade would receive twice as much as a child in the fifth grade, and a child in the ninth grade would receive three times as much as one

in the third grade. He also wants each child to have a bonus for good grades—10% to an A student, and 5% to a B student. His children are as follows:

Alice, 11th grade, A student
Bobby, 9th grade, B student
Carolyn, 6th grade, B student
Donald, 4th grade, A student
Elvira, 1st grade, C student

How should he distribute the $50?

(Answers on page 77)

Calculator Mathemetrics

The transition to the metric system, while it has been slow in coming, is certainly on its way, and your calculator will be helpful to you in making the adjustment. The conversion table below will help you put your best foot (make that .3048 meter) forward on the road to metrication. (Remember, many of the conversions shown give approximate rather than exact answers.)

LENGTH

Inches × 25.4   = Millimeters
Inches × 2.54   = Centimeters
Feet   × 30.48   = Centimeters
Feet   × 0.3048 = Meters
Yards × 91.44   = Centimeters
Yards × 0.9144 = Meters
Miles × 1.609   = Kilometers

AREA

Square Inches × 6.4516 = Square Centimeters
Square Feet   × 0.0929 = Square Meters
Square Yards × 0.8361 = Square Meters
Acres   × 0.4047 = Hectares
Square Miles × 2.59   = Square Kilometers

VOLUME

Cubic Inches × 16.387 = Cubic Centimeters
Cubic Feet   × 0.0283 = Cubic Meters
Cubic Yards × 0.7646 = Cubic Meters

CAPACITY

Dry Measure

Bushels × 35.238 = Liters

Liquid Measure

Fluid Ounces × 29.573 = Milliliters
Pints   × 473   = Milliliters
Pints   × 0.473 = Liters
Quarts   × 0.946 = Liters
Gallons   × 3.785 = Liters

WEIGHT

Ounces × 28.35 = Grams
Ounces ×   0.028 = Kilograms
Pounds × 453.59 = Grams
Pounds ×   0.454 = Kilograms
Tons   ×   0.91 = Metric Tons

TEMPERATURE

C = Celsius or Centigrade
(Fahrenheit degrees −32) × $\frac{5}{9}$ = Centigrade degrees
Centigrade degrees × 1.8 + 32 = Fahrenheit degrees

Now that you are a master of metric matters, here are a few problems to work with your calculator. See how you measure up.

1. If the standard of tallness is now 6 feet for a man, what will it be with metric?

2. If the standard of tallness for a woman is now 5 feet 9 inches, what will it be with metric?

3. If 200 pounds represents a husky man, what will be the metric standard?

4. If a person can run 100 yards in 10 seconds, how fast can he run 100 meters at the same average speed?

5. What race will replace the mile run? (Yes, the tracks will have to be changed.)

6. What standard will replace the four-minute mile on the new tracks?

7. If the speed limit is 55 m.p.h., what will it be in kilometers?

8. If a 6,980-yard golf course has par 70, and the holes are then remeasured in terms of meters, what would an appropriate par be?

9. If the size of a baseball diamond is increased from 30 yards to 30 meters, how would home run production be affected?

10. If a football place kicker can normally make 40% of his attempts from 50 yards out, what percentage should he make from 50 meters out?

11. Without rebuilding the course, what should the Indianapolis 500 be named?

12. What is the floor area of a room 20 feet × 15 feet, in metric?

13. If a zeppelin can hold 7,000,000 cubic feet of helium, what would be its metric capacity?

14. If potatoes cost 95¢ for 5 lbs., what would be a comparable package and price under metric?

15. If you can pole vault 18 feet, how well can you do in metric?

16. If you can long jump 18 feet, how well can you do in metric?

17. How much would a 12-lb. fish weigh in metric?

18. If you now take a deduction of 15¢ per mile on business use of your car for tax purposes, what will your deduction be in metric?

19. If you are flying 500 kilometers per hour against a 50 mile per hour headwind, how well could you do in calm air?

20. If you purchased 13.5 gallons of gasoline for $7.82, what would you expect to pay for a liter?

21. At what temperature are the values in Fahrenheit and Centigrade equal?

22. At what point is the Fahrenheit reading double the Centigrade?

23. At what point is the Centigrade reading double the Fahrenheit?

(Answers on page 78)

Treasure Hunt

Each guest or couple is given a number to put into a calculator. When turned upside down, this number will tell them the place to go to find the next clue. Well . . . almost. Remember that only a few letters of the alphabet can be represented by turning numbers upside down. Some of the letters in the clue will be missing, and the player will have to figure out what the complete word is. For instance, if the number 304373 came up in the display, the player would have to figure out that the clue is TELEPHONE.

When he solves the first clue and goes to the place indicated, he will find a new number which he must add or subtract to the number already in his machine, to get his next clue. Players had better write down each number as they come to it, which will make sure they discovered all the clues in order, and help them get back on the track if something should go wrong.

1.	773800	9.	−403571
2.	−770293	10.	+374523
3.	+704944	11.	−324773
4.	−708337	12.	+291894
5.	+700386	13.	−310443
6.	+71001	14.	+10097
7.	−399701	15.	+5525902
8.	+35578		

(Answers on page 79)

The Root of the Matter

A problem in square root is really a problem in division, with the special provision that the divisor is unknown, but must be the same figure as the quotient:

$$\begin{array}{r} 6 \\ \hline 6)\overline{36} \end{array}$$

Even if your calculator does not have a square root key, you can perform square root with only a few steps.

Let us take the square root of 3249. A quick estimate will tell you that the answer lies between 50 and 60. Let us take 55 as our first guess, and divide it:

$$\begin{array}{r} 59.072727 \\ \hline 55)\overline{3249} \end{array}$$

We have not fulfilled the condition that the divisor and quotient are the same figure, or even satisfactorily close. For our next estimate let us try a figure halfway between. This is found by adding the quotient and the divisor, and dividing by 2. This becomes our new divisor:

$$\begin{array}{r} 56.963663 \\ \hline 57.03636)\overline{3249} \end{array}$$

We now know that the correct answer lies somewhere between the quotient and the divisor. It is probably very close to 57, which is close enough for our purpose, and indeed happens to be the exact answer. If you wish, you can add the quotient and divisor again and divide by 2, and test this new figure out.

The ability to do square roots will enable you to do a variety of problems that otherwise would be quite difficult.

1. How far can you see across a body of water? Poor eyesight or hazy conditions might limit your vision, but ultimately everyone is limited by the same feature: the curva-

ture of the earth. The height of your eyes above the water is all-important. A rough formula, but accurate enough for most casual purposes, is $\sqrt{1.5H}$ where H represents your height in feet, and the answer comes out in miles. Suppose you are looking out from a tower 800 feet above the water. How far can you see to the horizon?

2. The formula for finding the length of the hypotenuse of a right triangle is that the square of the altitude plus the square of the base equal the square of the hypotenuse, or $A^2 + B^2 = H^2$. A $3 \times 4 \times 5$ triangle is often spoken of as a perfect triangle because:

$$3^2 + 4^2 = 5^2$$

Of course you could simply double the length of each side to find another perfect triangle. But can you find still another triangle, smaller than 15 on each side, in which the hypotenuse will also come out even?

3. How far should the bottom of a 16-foot ladder be placed from a wall in order to reach exactly 10 feet up the wall?

4. On a baseball diamond, the bases are 90 feet apart, and the pitching distance is 60.5 feet. Does the pitcher stand closer to home plate or second base?

(Answers on page 80)

Explosion!

The object of this game is to exceed the capacity of your calculator. Each player should have a calculator of similar capacity. Also required is a pair of dice. One die is of the standard kind. The other die has mathematical symbols pasted on its sides:

$$+ \quad - \quad \times \quad \div \quad N^x \quad (N^2)^2$$

Play begins with the first player putting 1 into his machine, then tossing the dice. If any of the first four symbols turns up, he will simply perform the mathematical operation indicated. For example, if he gets $\times$ and 6, he will multiply the number in his machine by 6. If at any time his display shows less than 1, he will begin again on his next turn.

If N^x turns up, he will raise the number in his display to the power indicated by the other die. For example, if he gets N^x and 4, he will multiply the number in his display by itself 3 times. (If you will notice, this is not the same thing as squaring his display 3 times.)

If $(N^2)^2$ turns up, the player will ignore the die with the numbers. Instead he will press the square key twice. If the calculator does not have a square key, he can accomplish the same thing by multiplying the number in the display by itself, then multiplying this product by itself.

The player who first "explodes" wins the game. A player who makes an error he cannot correct will start over on his next turn.

Variation 1. If a longer game is desired, use 0 instead of 1 as the starting point, or re-starting point.

Variation 2. If a much longer game is desired, substitute the $\sqrt{}$ for the $(N^2)^2$ notation.

Variation 3. If only one calculator is available, the players will all put their numbers and operations into the same machine, and the player who "explodes" the machine loses the game.

Strictly for Squares

1. Put the smallest number that you can into your calculator that is larger than 1 (1.00 . . . 1) and square it, then square your answer, and continue to do this. How many times can you perform this operation until you reach the capacity of your machine? Make a guess, before trying it out.

2. If you put a decimal that is smaller than 1 into your machine, then square it, and square your answer, and on indefinitely, what would be your final answer? Try to figure it out logically before trying it.

3. If you put a number larger than 1 into your machine, then take the square root, and take the square root of that, and so on indefinitely, what would be your final answer? Try to figure it out logically first.

4. If you put a decimal smaller than 1 into your machine, then took the square root of it, and took the square root of that, and so on indefinitely, what would be your final answer? Try to figure it out logically first.

(Answers on page 80)

More Upside-Down Displays

The rules for this section are the same as those on page 9.

a. $31 \times 11 \times 11$ and get a small island.

b. $3^9 + 35,495$ and get a description of married life.

c. $5,016 \times 11 + 2,542$ and get unwelcome arrivals on the first of the month.

d. $1,000 + 852.8667 \times 2$ and get the bottom line on your shoes.

e. $851^2 - 143,667$ and find what a man does when he loses a winning ticket worth $100,000.

f. $0 - 1,234,567 + 6,589,945$ and find what a preacher does.

g. $2,101 \times 18$ and get the name of a very good book.

h. $60^2 - 96$ and get a gardening tool.

i. $1,234 - 463$ and find out what you'll be after eating four gallons of ice cream.

j. $23^5 - 1,118,998$ and find what a woman does about her age.

k. $305,644 \div 43$ and get into hot water.

l. $9,999 - 8,038 \times 3$ and find what the tide does after it flows.

m. $73^2 + 9$ and get a honey of an answer.

n. $127^3 + 4,618,283 - 1,347,862$ and find how people occupy their spare time.

(Answers on page 81)

Three Complementary Lessons

SUBTRACTION

Many people believe that an adding machine accomplishes subtraction by having the wheels go around in the opposite direction. This was seldom true, even on the mechanical calculators that had wheels. Instead, subtraction is done by means of adding the complement. Complement means to complete. The complement of 149 is 851 because:

$$\begin{array}{r} 149 \\ +851 \\ \hline (1)000 \end{array}$$

Notice that the figures in each column total to 9, except in the final column which totals to 10. Note the following, however:

$$\begin{array}{r} 1094900 \\ +8905100 \\ \hline (1)0000000 \end{array}$$

Here it is the last column containing a significant figure that totals to 10. We are now ready for a subtraction problem:

$$\begin{array}{r} 738 \\ -149 \\ \hline 589 \end{array} \qquad\qquad \begin{array}{r} 738 \\ +851 \\ \hline (1)589 \end{array}$$

In the example above, your answer will be preceded by an unnecessary digit. This figure will tell you how many subtractions were made; in dealing with a column of figures there might be several subtractions among the additions.

ADDITION

It follows that if you can subtract by adding the complement, then you can add by subtracting the complement. $589 + 149 = 738$:

$$\begin{array}{r}(1)589\\-851\\\hline 738\end{array}$$

$$\begin{array}{r}589\\-851\\\hline -262\end{array}$$

You must cope with the extra digit which arises when we deal with complements. In the example at left, we incorporate this extra digit into the top number (the minuend). In the example at right, we must take the complement of the result, ignoring the minus sign, to arrive at the final answer.

DIVISION

You know that multiplication is really just multiple addition ($3 \times 4 = 3 + 3 + 3 + 3 = 12$), and, by the same token, division is nothing more than multiple subtraction. Let us divide, then, 18078 by 786, as follows:

$$\begin{array}{r}786\overline{)18078}\\-7860\\-7860\\-786\\-786\\-786\\\hline 0\end{array}$$

You keep subtracting in each set of columns until the answer showing in the display is smaller, in those particular columns, than your divisor (in this case, 786); then you move one position to your right. Your answer is 23, because you subtracted 2 times in the first available columns, then 3 times in the next available column.

It follows that if division is really subtraction, and subtraction is the same thing as adding the complement, then you could accomplish division by using only addition! And, while in the example above you had to keep track of the number of times you subtracted, the unwanted digits which crop up

33

when you do subtraction by adding complements will actually provide the answer to your division problem!

$$786\overline{)18078}$$

$+2140$	(a)
$\overline{20218}$	
$+2140$	(b)
$\overline{22358}$	(c)
$+214$	
$+214$	(d)
$\overline{22786}$	
$+214$	(e)
$\overline{23.000}$	(f)

The rules followed in this calculation are:

(a) 786 is larger than 180, so the complement will not be added in the first three columns. Move over one position, and add the complement the number of times shown in the first digit (1) of the dividend (18078).

(b) If this addition causes the first dividend digit to increase, as it did here, continue to add the complement until you "catch up" with it; in other words, until the number of additions equals the first digit of the new dividend.

(c) Now look at the next three digits (235 in this case). If this number is equal to or larger than the divisor (786), you must keep adding the complement until these three windows show a smaller figure than the divisor. Since 235 is less than 786, we do not add any more in these columns, but move one column to the right, just as we do in everyday division.

(d) In each new set of columns, we simply follow the same rules. First we add the complement the number of times shown in the window to the *immediate* left, which is 2 here, and is called the indicator. In our case, this addition did not cause the indicator to change.

(e) We now have 786 showing in the columns where we are working. Since this is equal to or larger than the divisor, we must add the complement again.

(f) Our answer is 23, the decimal point being moved three positions to the left to compensate for the three whole digits in the divisor. The 0's following the decimal point show that the problem came out even, and is finished. If there was a remainder, you could continue with the problem, but the decimal point will remain in its present position.

Family Finances

1. You deliver the daily newspaper, for which you get up very early, and also the Sunday newspaper, when you do not get up so early. The Sunday newspaper weighs about 4 times as much as the daily. A customer gives you a $1 Christmas tip, for which you properly thank him. This customer is a mathematician with a twinkle in his eye. Your sister delivers a weekly newspaper after school, weighing about ¼ as much as the daily newspaper. This customer, who also believes you should get a 25% bonus when you get up early, wants to tip your sister at exactly the same rate he tipped you with respect to the weight of the papers and the early-rising bonus. Should your sister thank him for his tip?

2. Dad is starting a new position, and has his choice of Plan A, where he will get a raise of $100 every 6 months, spread out over the following 6 months; or Plan B, where he will get a raise of $300 every year, spread out over the following year. Which is better?

(Answers on page 81)

Shopping Spree

Mom gives you a shopping list. It is proposed that you go to two different stores, and buy each item wherever it is cheaper. Of course you will only buy the minimum quantity that gives you the bargain price. Mom says she will give you all the money you save her, but she wants to see your calculations!

A. 20-ounce loaf of bread for 25¢, or 24-ounce loaf of bread for 29¢.

B. 6 28-ounce cans of tomatoes for $2.67, or 2 35-ounce cans for $1.19.

C. 2 10-ounce cans of peas for 69¢, or 6 8-ounce cans for $1.80.

D. Hamburger at 79¢/lb., or patties $\frac{1}{6}$ lb. each and packed 8 in a package at 99¢ a package.

E. Ice cream at $1.49 a half gallon, or 75¢ a quart.

F. 8 16-ounce bottles of pop for $1.19, or 6 28-ounce bottles for $1.30.

G. A 15-ounce box of crackers for 69¢, or a 2-pound box for $1.49.

H. 2 dozen plastic cups for 54¢, or 50 for $1.25.

I. 25 square feet of aluminum foil for 34¢, or 36 square feet for 59¢.

J. A 25-foot garden hose for $1.39, a 30-foot hose for $1.45, or a 50-foot hose for $2.36, and you need at least 75 feet.

K. A 5 × 7 color print for 75¢, or an 8 × 10 print for $2.50.

L. A 20-exposure color film for $2.43, or a 36-exposure color film for $3.84.

(Answers on page 82)

The Calculator Murders

Here is a list of the people who worked at the Acme Calculator Company:

Lise Bell	Bobo Hill
Hi Bishel	Elsie Lee (first victim)
Max Carty	Eli Shill
Lil Ellis (second victim)	Bob Sobel
Bill Hess	Ollie Sol

Two of the workers have been murdered. Police believe it is an inside job, and that the killer will strike again. Of course they could wait till everyone except one was murdered, and the person remaining would probably be the criminal, but this would involve considerable criticism of the police force. Besides, there is no firm evidence, and they would like to catch the dastardly villain in the act.

Can you help the police figure out the name of the fiend, his probable motive, and his next scheduled victim? Remember that murders, like wars, may be committed for very trivial reasons.

(Answer on page 83)

256	220	292	310	407	244	402	405	372	114	371	33	260	305	387
394	338	324	334	425	374	167	347	337	421	195	295	370	20	306
373	47	409	73	139	89	108	77	125	101	103	421	184	133	12
104	80	194	78	9	102	141	97	49	39	119	30	37	321	178
25	283	199	239	59						311	95	126	251	315
122	67	12	50	155						142	31	55	100	401
91	107	74	36	211						129	128	61	40	124
57	389	115	70	136						175	183	168	113	81
153	367	431	135	10	176	191	336	263	150	197	144	269	90	138
166	66	84	17	157	317	54	143	29	187	130	11	106	69	109
53	137	159	132	85	177	198	419	131	160	151	52	118	71	188
110	41	179	349	383	229	227	169	186	353	121	94	23	261	399
46	149	281	21	96	182	127	76	277	16	65	181	238	148	247
75	19	26	156	271	116	3	319	86	105	7	207	262	27	224
117	35	88	293	192	174	359	42	112	79	296	22	286	203	290
173	193	5	147	51	241	154	60	397	322	170	246	45	316	344
87	313	58	165	163	99	190	257	208	34	214	289	231	323	92
233	140	111	83	63	185	307	222	249	274	268	56	328	355	364
62	98	43	93	200	2	232	300	352	120	375	343	376	250	404
123	331	158	196	13	423	358	403	415	391	363	134	388	411	426
162	82	189	223	335	382	428	360	427	424	392	430	416	429	217

40

The Minotaur

Can you help the Minotaur escape through the labyrinth to one of the exits? The special hazard is that the monster has a mathematical head, and a deadly fear of prime numbers. He will gore anyone who attempts to lead him through such a block, bringing the problem to a premature end. No diagonal moves are permitted.

Which of these dozens of numbers are prime numbers? There are tables of prime numbers which you could consult, but why not figure it out for yourself? With your calculator in hand, it's an easy job.

As you may already know, a prime number is one that cannot be divided equally by any other number, except itself and 1. Although the number 1 would seem to fit this definition, it is usually excluded, because it does not lead to mathematically useful results. Let's test for prime numbers:

2 . . . yes, because it is our lowest number. (We can now exclude all other even numbers.)

3 . . . yes, because it is not equally divisible by 2.

5 . . . yes, because it is not equally divisible by 2 or 3. (We can now exclude all numbers ending in 5.)

7 . . . yes, because it is not equally divisible by 2, 3, or 5.

9 . . . no, because it is equally divisible by 3.

11 . . . yes, because it is not equally divisible by 2, 3, 5, or 7.

13 . . . yes, because it is not equally divisible by 2, 3, 5, 7, or 11.

17 . . . yes, because it is not equally divisible by 2, 3, 5, 7, 11, or 13.

19 . . . yes, because it is not equally divisible by 2, 3, 5, 7, 11, 13, or 17.

21 . . . no, because it is equally divisible by 3 and 7.

23 . . . yes, because it is not equally divisible by 2, 3, 5, 7, 11, 13, 17, or 19.

And so on.

Sometimes we will want to approach the problem from the other end. Is the number 517 prime? First let us take the square root of 517. Even if you do not have a square root key on your calculator, a little experimentation will show you that the answer is 22+. Therefore, if it is *not* a prime number, one of its factors must be 22 or smaller. Since we already know all the prime numbers under 25, all we need do is test these prime numbers to see if they will go into 517 evenly. It turns out that 11 is a factor, so 517 is not prime.

Now that you're well armed, see if you can rescue the Minotaur.

(*Answer on page 84*)

Much Ado About Decimals

You will feel much more at home with your calculator when working with decimals than with fractions. Nevertheless, some problems are stated in terms of fractions, and often you must change the fractions into decimals if you want your calculator to be of much help.

Changing a fraction into a decimal is usually quite simple. Divide the numerator by the denominator. $\frac{5}{8}$ is 5 divided by 8, which gives .625. Changing a decimal back into a fraction can be trickier, for decimals are of three kinds:

(1) Some decimals come to a firm end, like .625 above. This is easily converted to a fraction by putting 625 over 1000, and reducing it. $\frac{625}{1000} = \frac{5}{8}$. When this happens, you know that the fraction and the decimal are exactly equal. In all other cases, the decimal is not exactly the same as the fraction, because it extends on and on toward infinity. We take a sufficient number of decimal places to give us the degree of accuracy we need, and lop off the rest.

(2) Some decimals are never ending, never repeating. The value of pi or π is one such case. Pi is the ratio of the diameter of a circle to its circumference. If you multiply the diameter by pi, you will get the circumference, and this is true regardless of the size of the circle. For calculator purposes, we can call pi 3.1415926 . . . though the value has been carried out to a million places by computer. Mathematicians are able to prove that this number will never end, using our system of numbers and the necessary formula. With each additional position we

get a tiny bit closer to the exact point, but we can never quite reach it.

Some fractions will give a reasonably good approximation of pi. $\frac{22}{7}$ is sometimes used, which gives 3.1428571. An even better fraction is $\frac{355}{113}$, which gives 3.1415929, and ought to be good enough for almost any practical purpose.

(3) Some decimals are cyclical or repeating. If you change $\frac{1}{7}$ into a decimal, you will get .142857 142857 142857 . . . extending to infinity. Such a repeating decimal can be changed into a fraction by placing it over an equal number of 9's, and then reducing the fraction. (Why the denominator must consist of 9's would make an interesting math class demonstration.) The fraction $\frac{1}{3}$ gives the decimal .3333 . . . ; placing 3 over 9 gives the fraction $\frac{1}{3}$ again. The decimal .6666 . . . gives $\frac{6}{9}$ or $\frac{2}{3}$.

The decimal .142857 142857 . . . gives $\frac{142857}{999999}$ which reduces to $\frac{1}{7}$. You may have some trouble reducing such a fraction, for it contains some prime factors that are larger than you may be accustomed to dealing with, but your calculator will help. There is a short cut if you can assume the numerator is 1, for then the numerator will divide evenly into the denominator. If you can assume the numerator is 2, you can divide it by 2, and then it will go evenly into the denominator; and so on.

Handling a decimal such as .466666 . . . is a little trickier, since the repeating figure does not immediately follow the decimal point. Let us imagine the decimal to be .66666 . . . which gives $\frac{2}{3}$. But this decimal is preceded by a 4, which gives $\frac{12}{3}$. So now we have a total of $\frac{14}{3}$ preceded by a decimal point (if you can imagine such a grotesque number). The decimal point to the left of a number means that it has only $\frac{1}{10}$ the value you would ordinarily ascribe to it. You can eliminate the decimal point by multiplying the denominator by 10, which gives $\frac{14}{30}$, which reduces to $\frac{7}{15}$.

A repeating decimal arises from a fraction. How many digits can the repeating section have? It can have no more than the number appearing in the original denominator minus 1. Suppose you were changing $\frac{1}{7}$ into a decimal. You could carry the division out to as many places as you desired. Wherever you decided to stop, the remainder would have to be $\frac{1}{7}$, $\frac{2}{7}$, $\frac{3}{7}$, $\frac{4}{7}$, $\frac{5}{7}$, or $\frac{6}{7}$ After the decimal had been carried to 6 positions, you would then have to come to a remainder that you had already had before. Therefore, the decimal would repeat the same digits as it had once before when it had the same remainder.

Now try changing the fraction $\frac{1}{17}$ into a decimal. This would ordinarily be very simple: divide 1 by 17. But the answer will have 16 decimals, which then repeat, and we are assuming your calculator is not big enough to handle this figure. How can you find the entire repeating decimal?

If your calculator will show 7 decimal places, the problem would be done as follows:

```
          .0588235  2941176  4705882
17)1.0000000  0000000  0000000
   9999995
         5  0000000
         4  9999992
            8
```

Divide 1 by 17, and get the first 7 digits of your answer. Multiply this figure by 17, and then subtract it, getting a remainder of 5. You now have a new problem, that of $\frac{5}{17}$. Divide 5 by 17, and get the next 7 digits, multiply it out and get a remainder of 8. Your new problem is now $\frac{8}{17}$. The repeating decimal could have up to 16 places, and since this one does repeat after 16 places, you have a proof on your work. If you enjoyed this type of problem, you might want to try it for fractions with a denominator of 19, 23, 29, 47, 59, 61, or 97.

Problems to Tax You

1. Dad thinks his 1974 income tax may have been figured incorrectly, and wants you to recheck it. He paid $1,290 tax. His income was $13,262.76. In that year the government allowed 15% for deductions, and $750 for each exemption. Dad supports a wife and two children, and his mother who is over 65. The income tax Schedule Y for married taxpayers reads: "Over $4,000 but not over $8,000—$620 plus 19% of excess over $4,000." Was his tax correct?

2. A husband and wife filing jointly are entitled to a deduction up to $100 apiece on dividends received. If the husband's stock earned $145, and the wife's stock earned $18, and the jointly held stock earned $68, what is their deduction?

3. Sam Sadde earns $100 for a 40-hour week. His deductions for one week were:

Federal income tax	$7.80
State income tax	$.31
City income tax	1.5%
Social security	5.85%
Retirement fund	10%
Hospitalization insurance	$11.54
Union dues	$2.00
Office flower fund	$.50
United Appeal	$.04
Garnishee	15%
Accommodation with creditors	7.5%
Support for two children	$15.00 each
Payment on loan from employer	$10.00
Personal use of company car 197 miles @ 15¢	
Due on credit union loan	$13.50

U.S. bonds	$2.50
Christmas fund	$1.00
Newspaper delivery	$.75

He gets paid time and a half for overtime. How many hours should he work next week if he wants to double his take-home pay? Assume his car mileage will remain the same, and there will be no federal or state tax deductions.

(Answers on page 85)

Timely Problems

1. Mom and Dad ask you to settle a dispute. Mom watches TV about 2 hours a day, and spends about 1 hour on the telephone. Dad watches TV about 1 hour a day, and practically never talks on the phone at home. Each sleeps 8 hours a night. Dad must spend 60 hours a week away from home, and Mom must spend 15 hours a week away from home. Which spends the greater percentage of waking time at home on TV and telephoning?

2. Mom says she will cut her television time, so she has the same total percentage as Dad. How long can she watch in a week?

3. Have you lived 1,000,000,000 seconds yet?

4. A car in the Indianapolis 500 has completed the first hundred laps (250 miles) at an average speed of 150 m.p.h. What speed must it maintain to average 160 m.p.h. for the entire race?

5. A man buys a new camera for $500, with the expectation that he will eventually take 5,000 pictures with it. His usual exposure time is $\frac{1}{100}$ second. What is the cost of his camera per minute of exposure?

(Answers on page 86)

Magicalculations

One of the most useful tricks in the magician's repertoire is the ability to "force" a card. The magician asks a volunteer to select a card at random, but, through sleight of hand, the card picked is the one the magician wants to be chosen. To perform magic on the calculator, you don't have to master difficult manipulations with your hands—the only digits you will manipulate are the ones in your calculator display. These tricks are the easiest kind of magic, since they will work themselves once you know the mathematical secrets involved.

1. You can allow your friend to choose any random number, of any number of digits, and force him to arrive at the number 9. Simply have him choose his number, then scramble the digits and subtract. Then have him cross-add the digits until he has only one digit. This digit will always be 9! Here is one example.

$$\begin{array}{r} 567134 \\ -341765 \\ \hline 225369 = 27 = 9 \end{array}$$

You could stop the trick here, and simply guess the number 9, but why not make things more interesting. If you know your friend's age or street address, you can have him add or subtract until he reaches it. Probably the most impressive way to perform this trick is to write down a prediction on a slip of paper before the trick begins and hand it to a spectator. Then have your friend add to the 9 he will reach until he matches your prediction, and ask to have the prediction read aloud.

One more idea which will make the trick even more astounding. The random number which is scrambled in the first step can be the product of any number of random numbers, and

any assortment of operations. Hence, your friend can start with any number, multiply, divide, add or subtract at will, then perform the scrambling, subtracting and cross-adding, and you will *still* know that his result is 9.

2. Another quick way to "force" a 9 on your unsuspecting friend is to give him the following directions:

"Put into your calculator any number with two different digits."

28

"Reverse the digits and subtract the smaller from the larger."

82
54

"Divide by the difference in your original two digits." (in this case, 6)

9

You will get the same result by simply subtracting the reversed digit number from the original, as long as you tell your friend to ignore the negative sign.

You won't want to do the trick the same way every time, and of course you must keep things moving fast enough so your audience won't realize that a 9 is coming up all the time. Here are some other methods:

"Take a random number up to seven digits." 4751
"Multiply by 10." 47510
"Subtract your original number." 42759
"Divide by your original number." 9

or

"Take a random number up to six digits." 4751
"Multiply by 100." 475100
"Subtract your original number." 470349
"Divide by 11." 42759
"Divide by your original number." 9

3. This stunt works well for a friend whose age you do not know. First memorize the number 43,046,721, or have it

written on a slip of paper in your pocket. Then ask your friend to perform the following:

"Put in the year of your birth."

"Subtract 3."

"Add your age."

"If you have not had your birthday this year, add 1." (Omit if you know his birthday is past.)

"Subtract the current year."

"Add 6."

"Square the amount in our machine."

"Square it again."

"Square it again."

"Square it again."

Then you tell him the answer, or produce the paper from your pocket. The secret is that when he put in the year of his birth, plus his age this year, and subtracted the current year, nothing remained. All that your machine contained was $-3 + 6 = 3$. Knowing there will be a 3 in the machine, you then carry out any previously determined calculation you please.

4. Sometimes you will want your friend to select a secret number, go through some calculations, and return to the secret number. Multiplying a number by .625 is of course the same thing as multiplying by $\frac{5}{8}$. To revert back to your original number, multiply by 8 and divide by 5.

MAIL / ROOM

TRAINEE

| 2 | 3 | 4 | 5 | 6 | 7 | 8 | 9 | 10 |

11

CLERK

| 21 | 20 | 19 | 18 | 17 | 16 | 15 | 14 | 13 | 12 |

22

CHIEF ACCOUNTANT

| 23 | 24 | 25 | 26 | 27 | 28 | 29 | 30 | 31 | 32 |

33

BRANCH OFFICE MANAGER

| 43 | 42 | 41 | 40 | 39 | 38 | 37 | 36 | 35 | 34 |

44

MAIN OFFICE MANAGER

| 45 | 46 | 47 | 48 | 49 | 50 | 51 | 52 | 53 | 54 |

55

TREASURER

| 65 | 64 | 63 | 62 | 61 | 60 | 59 | 58 | 57 | 56 |

66

VICE PRESIDENT OF THINGAMAJIGS

| 67 | 68 | 69 | 70 | 71 | 72 | 73 | 74 | 75 | 76 |

VICE PRESIDENT OF GOBBLEDYGOOK 77

| 87 | 86 | 85 | 84 | 83 | 82 | 81 | 80 | 79 | 78 |

88

PRESIDENT

CHAIRMAN OF THE BOARD

| 89 | 90 | 91 | 92 | 93 | 94 | 95 | 96 | 97 |

Climbing the Corporate Calculadder

The object of this game is to move from the Mail Room to the office of Chairman of the Board. Each player, in his turn, draws a card and moves either forward or backwards, using his calculator to follow the instructions on the card. The game is played on the board at left. To make a set of cards, either copy the information on pages 54–56 onto individual cards, or photocopy the page, mount the copy on a sheet of cardboard, and cut into individual cards.

Each player has a token or marker of some kind, and begins the game in the Mail Room. The first two lines on the board, "Trainee" and "Clerk," are non-executive lines, and may be occupied by any number of players. Each remaining line, however, is an executive suite, and *the entire line* may be occupied by only one player at a time. The shaded squares, number 22, 33, 44 and so on, are waiting squares, and may also be occupied by only one player at a time.

A player who cannot complete a forward move because he would land in an occupied suite must stay in the waiting square before the suite, until his directions allow him either to advance to an unoccupied suite or force him to retreat. If the executive suite to which a player would retreat is occupied, he must continue to retreat until he lands in an unoccupied waiting square or a non-executive suite. Of course, a player can pass through an occupied suite if his move permits him to reach an unoccupied executive suite or waiting square beyond.

It is not necessary to reach the final square, Chairman of the Board, on an exact number of moves. However, no player may become Chairman of the Board while the office of the President is occupied by an opponent.

Following are several suggested sets of directions for your cards. You may, of course, make up other directions as you please.

If you are on a prime number, advance to the next prime number. If not, retreat to the preceding prime number.	You will owe $100 income tax on April 15. If, by saving $1 on every working or school day, you will be able to pay your tax, advance 10 spaces; if not, retreat 5.
You may exchange places with any opponent, provided he is not on a prime number.	Place a random whole number in your calculator, and multiply by a number called off by the player to your left. Advance by the number of the digit showing in the hundreds column.
If you are on a square number, advance to . the next available square number, but do not advance through an occupied executive suite.	Reverse the digits in your age, subtract 20, and go to that square (ignore − sign).
Add the digits in your local telephone number. Then separately add the digits in your present age, and multiply by 3. If the first is larger, subtract the second and advance that number of squares. If the second is larger, subtract the first and retreat.	If the street number of your house or apartment is such that every digit can be found in your telephone number, advance 3 squares.

Take or estimate the square root of the number you are on, ignoring the decimal. If it is 5 or less, advance that number of squares. If it is more than 5, retreat that number.	Take your hat size (if you don't know it, take 7), multiply by your shoe size, add your waist size, and divide by the number of people in your family. If a 9 appears in the display, advance 9 spaces.
Cross-add the digits in your birthdate—month, day, and year, and if that number on the board is not in an occupied suite, go to it. Otherwise, retreat 5 spaces.	Take your weight, divide by your height in inches, and advance the number of whole squares indicated.
Take your age and your best friend's age, add them, then square them. then add the odd digits in your answer and advance that number of squares.	Place a random eight-digit figure in your calculator, add an eight-digit figure called off by the player to your left. If the answer contains two matching digits next to each other, advance by that digit; if there is more than one combination, advance by all of them.
Take the present Fahrenheit temperature outside, change it to Centigrade, and go to this square or as close as you can get. (F. degrees −32) × 5/9 = C. degrees.	Multiply together the present numbers of all the players. If your answer is equally divisible by 13, 17, or 19, advance by that number. If it is equally divisible by 3, 5, or 7, retreat this number of spaces. You may have to do both.

55

Add together the present numbers of all players. If you get a prime number, advance to the next waiting square, but do not pass through an occupied executive suite. If you do not get a prime number, find the lowest divisor and retreat this number.

Divide $100 by the number of shopping days till Christmas, and advance by the number to the left of the decimal point. If less than $1.00, retreat by the first digit to the right of the decimal point.

Place a four-digit random number in your machine, and multiply by a four-digit random number called off by the player to your left. Find the largest repeated digit in the answer, and advance this number. If no digit is repeated, advance 25 squares.

If the number you are on is exactly divisible by 4.25, advance 17 spaces. If not, retreat 1 space.

Take the first letter in your auto license and calculate its position in the alphabet. If it is a consonant, advance that number; if a vowel, retreat. If your license has only digits, don't move.

Problems of Interest

1. If you invested some money at 4% interest, compounded annually, in what year would your money double itself? At 5%? At 6%? At 8%? At 10%?

2. Dad has a mortgage of $10,000 at 9% interest, on which he pays $300 per month. In how many months will the mortgage be paid off? Now of course you could take his payment each month, divide it as to interest and principal, then figure his new balance. But there is an easier way, requiring only one multiplication a month, and the multiplier is always the same.

3. Dad says he already knew the answer to that, because he checked with the bank. But now that he has more confidence in you, what would it be if he raised his monthly payments to $400?

4. Mom bought merchandise costing $100, and offered payment, but the merchant handed back $5, saying that represented a discount for cash. But Mom refused the money, saying she would prefer to have a $5 gift certificate for a friend. Did she cheat herself?

5. You borrowed $1 from a friend, and exactly a month later paid him back $1.10. What annual rate of interest did you pay?

6. Dad borrowed $1,200 from a bank and paid back $106 a month for a year. What rate of interest did he pay?

(Answers on page 86)

Home Improvements

1. What will it cost to carpet an 18-foot × 13-foot living room, a 14-foot × 14-foot dining room, and a 14½-foot × 3½-foot hall, at $7.50 per square yard? Figure that 10% of the material will be wasted due to cutting.

2. A paperhanger offers to hang a room 20 feet × 12 feet × 9 feet for a price of $125 for his time alone. He allows nothing off for openings or baseboards. If you decide to have the ceiling painted instead of papered, and he can paint in about ⅓ the time, what should his fee now be?

3. The house shown in the illustration is 38 feet tall, which includes gables of 10 feet and a brick foundation of 3 feet above the ground. The other dimensions are 28 feet × 22 feet. A painter wants to earn 20¢ per square foot, and he will allow nothing off for doors and windows because he says it is as hard to paint around them as over them. What should he estimate? (The area of a triangle equals ½ base times height.)

4. You have a dripping faucet which wastes 1 gallon of water every 20 hours. You call in a plumber, who looks at the problem and asks for $20 to fix it. He estimates the repair will last five years. Water costs you $4.39 per 1,000 cubic feet. Does it pay to have him fix the faucet? (There are 231 cubic inches in a gallon.)

5. You have a 50-foot by 75-foot lawn, and want to water it for the equivalent of a ¼-inch rain. What will it cost at the above rates?

6. A customer has his choice of two identical water heaters, both priced at $100. The first carries a full five-year warranty. The second carries a ten-year warranty, but on a sliding scale: $100 the first year, $90 the second year, and so on. Which is the better buy?

(Answers on page 88)

FREEDOM

Column markers: 1   2   3   4

Col 1	Col 2 (PRISON)	Col 3	Col 4
+11	×6	×4	×3
N^2	N^2	N^2	N^2
÷7	÷7	÷7	÷7
×45	×45	×45	×45
−5	−5	−5	−5
−6	−6	−6	−6
×3	×3	×3	×3
÷2	÷2	÷2	÷2
+8	+8	+8	+8
×2	×2	×2	×2
−6	−6	−6	−6
×1	×1	×1	×1

Calculated Risk

"Shifty" Dijitz, a mathematically talented criminal, has planned an escape through a series of tunnels which run under the prison walls. He has made up a map, shown at left, which represents the degree of risk involved in each possible pathway to freedom. The warden has found the map, but cannot figure out what route Dijitz will follow. Can you?

The object is to make as low a total score as possible, representing the smallest possible risk. With each block you enter, you must make the indicated mathematical calculation on your calculator.

For example, you may decide to start with the digit 1 at the top of the diagram. (This might or might not be correct.) You will enter 1 in your calculator. The next block you go to says $+11$, so you will add this amount, making 12. What shall you do next? You might proceed straight through this tunnel, entering the block which reads N^2, which means you square the amount in your calculator, making 144, and on the next block divide by 7. But instead of entering N^2, you may decide to take a detour into the side tunnel, subtracting 14, dividing by 59 and so forth, in hopes of lowering the number in your display.

No block may be entered more than once, and if you have advanced towards the outside, you cannot retreat towards the prison. There are thousands of possible courses, so obviously it is not practical to try them all. Approaching the problem with some logic will reduce the possibilities to manageable proportions.

(*Answer on page 89*)

More Magicalculations

1. Here is a simple trick which is especially good for displaying your friend's street address or the last 4 digits of his telephone number. Suppose his address is 3823. Before the trick, secretly subtract 1089 from this number:

$$\begin{array}{r} 3823 \\ -1089 \\ \hline 2734 \end{array}$$

Now ask your friend to perform the following:

"Choose a three-digit number."	235
"Reverse the digits and subtract the smaller from the larger."	$\dfrac{532}{297}$
"Do you now have a three-digit number?" (If he answers "Yes") "Reverse the digits and add."	$\begin{array}{r} 792 \\ \hline 1089 \end{array}$
"Add 2734."	3823

Ask him if this number has any significance, and he will be startled to admit it is his own address!

There are only two things to keep in mind while doing this trick. If, after the initial calculation, there is not a three-digit number in the machine, then tell your friend to "Reverse the digits, put a zero on the end, and add." The number he had gotten was 99 (403 − 304, 322 − 223, etc.) and adding 990 yields 1089.

The other possibility is that the initial calculation will lead to zero, as 828 − 828, or 383 − 383. These are called "palindromic numbers": caution him about them and start over.

2. Here is another device for forcing your friend to "choose" any digit you want him to. If you multiply 1001 (or $7 \times 11 \times 13$) $\times$ 111 (or 3×37) $\times$ 9 (or 3×3), you will get 999999. Ask your friend to select any digit between 2 and 6, multiply by $1001 \times 111 \times 9$, and divide by 7, and he will get the number 142857, in varied order. You can now get him to select a digit of your own choice by telling him to take the lowest digit (1), or the lowest even digit (2), or the sum of the two lowest digits (3), or the lowest even digit doubled (4), or the middle-sized odd digit (5), or the sum of the two lowest digits times 2 (6), or the highest odd digit (7), or the highest digit (8), or the sum of the two lowest digits times 3 (9).

Since you know what digit he will choose, you can now carry him through some involved calculation to which you already know the answer. If the calculator has a memory, you can do this other calculation first, put it aside in memory, then retrieve it later for more hokus-pokus.

There is another interesting property of the number 142,857. If you multiply this number by any digit between 1 and 6, you will get a number containing exactly the same digits in a different order as your result.

3. There are many other devices that will lead your unsuspecting friend to get a number into the calculator that you already know. He can select any secret three-digit number and multiply by 1001 ($7 \times 11 \times 13$), and the secret number will duplicate, side by side. We can now work the stunt in reverse. Ask him to select a secret three-digit number, and duplicate it side by side. We now know that the secret number $\times 7 \times 11 \times 13$ will equal the number now in the machine. If we want him to have 13 left, we will ask him to divide by 7 and 11 and his secret number. If we want 77 left, we will ask him to divide by

13 and the secret number. If we want the secret number left, we will divide by 7 and 11 and 13. If we want a 1 left, we will divide by all four numbers.

The same stunt can be worked with two-digit numbers. Ask your friend to select a secret two-digit number, and to triplicate it side by side. This is the same as multiplying by 10101 (factors $3 \times 7 \times 13 \times 37$). You can divide out as before.

To work the stunt with a one-digit number, ask him to triplicate it side by side. This is the same as multiplying by 111 (factors 3×37), and proceed as before.

Where There's a Will

1. Cal Q. Later passed away recently. In his last will and testament, he specified that $\frac{1}{2}$ of his estate was to go to his wife, $\frac{1}{3}$ to his son, $\frac{1}{7}$ to his daughter, and the remainder to his dog. Before the estate could be distributed, the dog ran away, and has not been heard of since. What percentage of the estate should the three remaining heirs receive?

2. In his last will and testament, Abe E. Sea left 25% of his wealth to charity. He left 50% of the remainder to his wife, and 12% of the remainder after that to each of his two sons. The balance of $11,400 went to his daughter. What was the total amount of his estate?

(Answers on page 91)

Oranges and Doughnuts

1. Henry Ernest Dudeney has a well-deserved reputation as one of the foremost British puzzlers. This problem which he published is presented partly to introduce his work, and partly because it was quite tedious then, but should be fun with a calculator.

A groceryman wants to stack up a pile of oranges, in the form of a square pyramid. That is, the top layer will have 1 orange (which is not the answer to the problem), the next layer will have 4 oranges (2 × 2), the next layer 9 oranges (3 × 3), and so on. The layers are to be continued until the total number of oranges in the pyramid is a square number. (To remind you, a square number is one that results when a smaller number is multiplied by itself.) Just to make sure you will not go too far astray, let us stipulate that the correct answer is below 10,000.

2. Have you ever heard of Sam Loyd, the brilliant American puzzler? Perhaps not, but you've surely seen his work. Have you ever played Parcheesi? Have you ever seen a pencil with a loop of string attached, and even though the loop is too small to pass over the other end of the pencil, it can still be attached to a buttonhole? Have you ever fooled with the impossible little puzzle (though many people claim to have solved it) which consists of little blocks sliding around in a square frame, the blocks numbered from 1 to 15 with one blank space? The numbers are in order except that 14 and 15 are interchanged, and the problem is to get them back into the right order. All this is Loyd's work. Here is one of his problems, and we can be forgiven for changing a grindstone into doughnuts, because

who can eat a grindstone? A baker has a 10-inch circle of flat dough, with a 1-inch circle already cut out of the middle. His problem is to cut the remaining dough so he will make 2 doughnuts, one inside the other, with each containing the same amount of dough. (Remember that the area of a circle equals πr^2. If your calculator shows eight digits, use $\pi = 3.1415926$ in your calculations.)

(Answers on page 92)

What Is Going On Inside?

It is possible to drive a car without knowing very much about the engine, and it is possible to use a calculator without knowing very much about what is happening inside. But isn't it more fun to know? This knowledge becomes vital if you enter the field of computer designing, repairing, or programming.

In a computer each tiny bit of information can be charged electrically or magnetically. It is either on or off, charged or not charged. Therefore, a computer can use only two digits, 1 and 0. This is called the binary or base 2 system, as contrasted with our base 10 system. You put in your number in base 10, the computer transforms it to base 2 and performs the calculation, then transforms the answer back into base 10 for you to see.

How can we transfer our number 1,000,000 into a base 2 number? Perhaps the easiest way to accomplish this, if you have only a few such numbers, is to divide the number continuously by 2. Sometimes you will have 1 left over, and if so put it off to the side. You will note that you have a 1 after every odd number.

```
1000000
 500000
 250000
 125000
  62500
  31250
  15625  1
   7812
   3906
   1953  1
    976
    488
    244
    122
     61  1
     30
     15  1
      7  1
      3  1
      1  1
```

The base 2 number is found by reading the remainder column up from the bottom, filling the empty places with 0's:

11110100001001000000

How can we prove the value of the above number? Use the following table:

524288	262144	131072	65536	32768	16384	8192	4096	2048	1024	512	256	128	64	32	16	8	4	2	1
1	1	1	1	0	1	0	0	0	0	1	0	0	1	0	0	0	0	0	0

Wherever a 1 appears on the bottom line, add in the number at the top:

$$
\begin{array}{r}
524288 \\
262144 \\
131072 \\
65536 \\
16384 \\
512 \\
\underline{64} \\
1000000
\end{array}
$$

The table will also show that 1000000 in base 2 is the same as 64 in base 10.

This table can also be useful if you have very many base 10 numbers to change into base 2. Suppose the number to be changed is 675. Subtract the largest number on the table that you can, then from your new number continue to subtract the largest number available. From the table, put a 1 below every number you used for subtraction, and a 0 in all the other positions.

$$
\begin{array}{r}
675 \\
-512 \\
\hline
163 \\
-128 \\
\hline
35 \\
-32 \\
\hline
3 \\
-2 \\
\hline
1 \\
-1 \\
\hline
\end{array}
$$

Your answer would be: 1010100011.

Here is how your base 2 calculator would handle a problem in addition:

8	1000
4	100
5	101
2	10
19	(1211)
	10011

Actually your calculator cannot handle the 2 in the number 1211, which is included only for purposes of illustration, but transforms it into 10011. Can you figure out the rule for making this change? In a base 10 system, if we have 10 too much, we carry it as 1 into the column to the left; but in base 2, if we have 2 too much, we carry it as 1 into the column to the left. Start from the right, and if the digit is 1 or 0, allow it to stand. But if it is 2, show 0 below, and carry 1 to the left. If a 3 appears, show it as 1, and carry 1 to the left. If a 4 appears, show it as 0, and carry 2 to the left; and so on.

Fuelish Figures

1. Gas gives 1,040 British Thermal Units per cubic foot, and costs $1.625 per thousand cubic feet. Coal gives 15,000 B.T.U. per pound, and costs $25 per ton. Fuel oil gives 142,500 B.T.U. per gallon, and costs 35¢ per gallon. Electricity gives 1,000 B.T.U. per .2928 kilowatt hours, and costs 4¢ per kwh. Which is the most economical fuel?

2. If an electric clock is rated at 1.7 watts, how much does it cost to run it for 30 days at the above rates?

3. If a frost-free refrigerator uses 15 kwh. in 3 days, what is the cost to run it for 30 days at the above rates?

4. If the pilot lights in a home use 1 cubic foot in 14 minutes, what is the cost of running them for 30 days at the above rates?

(Answers on page 93)

Peasant Multiplication

Multiplication is nothing more than addition. If you wish to multiply 786 × 23, you could take 786 and add it 23 times, or you could take 23 and add it 786 times. This would prove very tedious, and where fatigue sets in, errors increase. Where the same number is to be added many times, multiplication provides a short cut, because you can memorize certain number combinations, i.e., your multiplications tables. These memories can be programmed into a computer. In our problem here, we are imagining that these tables are not available.

On your machine you could of course take 786 and add it 23 times, which would be less tedious than mental computation. But a short cut is available. You need add 786 only 3 times, and 7860 only twice:

$$
\begin{array}{r}
786 \\
786 \\
786 \\
7860 \\
\underline{7860} \\
18078
\end{array}
$$

There is a fascinating traditional system for multiplying, called Peasant Multiplication, which requires only the ability to halve and double, rather than memorizing complicated multiplication tables.

Peasant Multiplication is a system which is easy to work but hard to explain. Let us suppose that you want to multiply 39 × 71. But you do not know the multiplication tables beyond the 2's, and you certainly don't want to go through a long addition problem. Instead, you head two columns with 39 and 71. In the first column you continually divide by 2, ignoring any remainders, and in the second column you constantly double the preceding figure. You check off the odd numbers in the first column, pick up the figure in the second column, and enter it in the third column. The total of the third column is your answer.

39	71	71
19	142	142
9	284	284
4	568	
2	1136	
1	2272	2272
		2769

But how does it work? Try to figure it out for yourself and, if you're really stumped, see the answer on page 93.

Car-ful Calculations

1. You have your choice of buying a new car for $5,000, or a used car of the same model that is 2 years old for $3,000. It is estimated that in the first year a new car is covered by warranty, and in the second year repairs would be negligible. But in the third year repairs would come to $100, and the repair bill would increase by 50% every year thereafter. Whichever car you buy, you intend to keep it until it has no trade-in value to speak of. Assume that these prices will all remain stable for many years ahead, that repairs are of no particular inconvenience to you except for the money involved, that you are not concerned about carrying charges because you will pay cash, and you are not thinking about bank interest you may be losing, because if you didn't spend your money on this you would be spending it on something else. Is it more economical to buy the new car or the used car, and how long should you keep it?

2. Gasoline in your state costs 55¢ a gallon at your local service station, but you can get it for 50¢ across the state border, 17 miles away. Your car normally makes 17 miles per gallon. How many gallons would you have to buy to make the trip across the state border worthwhile? Time and depreciation are of no importance, because your family enjoys riding.

(Answers on page 94)

Answers

Upside-Down Displays

a. HI
b. OBOE
c. EEL
d. HE IS BOSS
e. SHELL OIL
f. ESSO OIL
g. SILO
h. SOS
i. LOBO
j. BELLE
k. HISSES
l. HILL
m. HELLO
n. LOLLI (POP)
o. HOHOHO

Sports Figures

1. If you take $5 \div 2 + 15 \div 2 + 15 \div 2 \ldots$ you will find that the ball is destined to approach but never touch the 15- and 30-yard lines. With each exchange of penalties it comes closer.

2. It is easy to see that with every 12 games played, you will break even if Mudville wins 5, because

$$5 \times 7\cent = 7 \times 5\cent$$

Because 156 divided by 12 is 13, you must multiply the games above by 13.

$$65 \times 7¢ = 91 \times 5¢$$

In this way we can see that the Mudville Nine won 65 games.

3. Babe Ruth hit a home run every 2.57 games. Roger Maris hit a home run every 2.66 games. So Ruth was ahead, but was perhaps less fatigued from the shorter season!

Making Allowances

1. You might begin by putting 1 into your machine (rather than .01) because your calculator may drop the extra decimals without your realizing it. In any case, if you have an 8-digit calculator, and double the sum continuously, on the 27th day your display will read 67108864. If you double again you will exceed its capacity. You can get around this difficulty by taking the first four digits and doubling them the required number of times, then the last four digits, combining your answers. The amount you will earn on the 30th day is $5,368,709.12. But you still have the problem of adding your earnings for all 30 days. Must you do this tediously, or is there a short cut? Notice that your earnings on any given day will be 1¢ larger than your total earnings of all the previous days. Therefore, you can take the amount earned on the 30th day, double it, and subtract 1¢, for an answer of $10,737,418.23.

2. Under proposition (b) you will only earn $4.65. Under proposition (c) put 1 into your machine and multiply by 1.03 continuously. On the 15th day your earnings will exceed 1½¢, and so will become 2¢, but they will never reach 3¢ in a month. Therefore, your earnings are:

14 days @ 1¢	.14
16 days @ 2¢	.32
	.46

3. The children's allowances are figured as follows:

Alice	11 parts + 10% = 12.1 parts		$18.20
Bobby	9 parts + 5% = 9.45 parts		14.21
Carolyn	6 parts + 5% = 6.3 parts		9.47
Donald	4 parts + 10% = 4.4 parts		6.62
Elvira	1 part	1 part	1.50
Total		33.25 parts	$50.00

Alice's share would be 12.1 ÷ 33.25 × 50.

Calculator Mathemetrics

1. About 183 cm.
2. About 175 cm.
3. About 91 kg.
4. About 10.94 seconds.
5. A mile equals about 1,600 meters, but a more likely choice is to use a round number, in this case 1,500.
6. About 3 minutes 44 seconds.
7. About 88.5 k.p.h.
8. 70—metric won't help your golf score, unless the length of the holes is changed.
9. Assuming the size of the diamond alone is changed, not the ballpark itself, the change would have little effect on home runs. Most are hit out of the park and, while it would be slightly harder to make home runs inside the park, these are quite rare.
10. It would be dangerous to assume that because of the slightly longer distance his successes would fall off in the same proportion. Maybe 50 yards represents the limit of his ability, and 50 meters (about 55 yards) would be too much and he would never make them.

11. The Indianapolis 805 (kilometers, approximately).
12. About 28 square meters.
13. About 198,000 cubic meters.
14. Around $2\frac{1}{4}$ kilograms, priced at about 95¢.
15. Almost $5\frac{1}{2}$ meters.
16. Almost $5\frac{1}{2}$ meters.
17. About $5\frac{1}{2}$ kilograms, allowing for a slight fish story.
18. About 9.3 cents per kilometer.
19. About 580 kilometers per hour.
20. About 15.3¢, rounding off in your favor, as you might hope.
21. -40 degrees.
22. 160 degrees Fahrenheit equals 320 degrees Centigrade.
23. -12.3 degrees Fahrenheit equals -24.6 degrees Centigrade, approximately.

Treasure Hunt

1. DOORBELL
2. 3507 = CLOSET
3. 708451 = FISHBOWL
4. 114 = HI-FI
5. 700500 = FOOTSTOOL
6. 771501 = WINDOWSILL
7. 371800 = AUTOMOBILE
8. 407378 = TABLECLOTH
9. 3807 = GLOBE
10. 378330 = COFFEE TABLE
11. 53557 = GLASSES
12. 345451 = DISHWASHER
13. 35008 = BOOKCASE
14. 45105 = SOAPDISH
15. 5571007 = LOOKING GLASS

The Root of the Matter

1. The square root of (1.5 × 800) comes to about 34.64 miles. Can you see why this formula would not work on the moon?

2. $5^2 \times 12^2 = 13^2$.

3. About 12.49 feet.

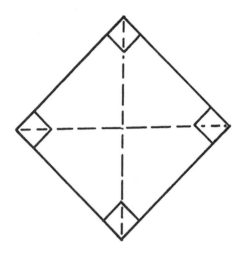

4. If you think of the diamond as four right triangles butted together as shown above, you can easily find the distance to the center of the field. By taking the square root of 4050 ($90^2 \div 2$) you find that the center of the field is about 63.64 feet from all bases, and so the pitcher stands closer to home plate.

Strictly for Squares

1. If you have an eight-digit calculator, 27 times.

2. Your answer would tend towards 0.

3. Your answer would tend towards 1.

4. Your answer would tend towards 1.

More Upside-Down Displays

a. ISLE
b. BLISS
c. BILLS
d. HEEL, SOLE
e. HE SOBS
f. BLESSES
g. BIBLE
h. HOSE
i. ILL
j. SHE LIES
k. BOIL
l. EBBS
m. BEES
n. HOBBIES

Family Finances

1. Let us say that the daily paper weighs 1 quiblon, and the Sunday paper weighs 4 quiblons. The daily papers in a week weigh 6 quiblons, plus a 25% bonus means you will get credit for 7.5 quiblons. The total weight for the week comes to 11.5 quiblons, of which 4 applies to Sunday. $4 \div 11.5 \times \$1$ gives 34.78¢ of your tip which applies to the Sunday paper. Your sister's weekly paper weighs $\frac{1}{16}$ as much as the Sunday paper, and since no bonus applies to Sunday, she should receive $\frac{1}{16}$ as much as your Sunday tip, or 2.17¢. Of course she should thank him, for politeness never costs anything, and if he actually gave her 3¢ she should thank him warmly for his generosity.

2. Plan A is substantially better. The following table shows how much:

| | Plan A | | Plan B | Net Gain Under |
	6 mo.	6 mo.	year	Plan A
First year	0	100	0	100
Second year	200	300	300	200
Third year	400	500	600	300
Fourth year	600	700	900	400
Fifth year	800	900	1200	500
Total gain in 5 years				$1500

Shopping Spree

A. The second is cheaper by $.0004167 per ounce × 48

Savings 2¢

B. The first is cheaper by $.0011072 per ounce, × 168

Savings 19¢

C. The first is cheaper by $.003 per ounce, × 20   Savings 6¢

D. The second is cheaper by $.0475 per pound, × 1⅓

Savings 6¢

E. The first is cheaper by 1¢ a half gallon   Savings 1¢

F. The second is cheaper by $.0015588 per ounce, × 168

Savings 26¢

G. The first is cheaper by $.0005625 per ounce, × 15

Savings 1¢

H. The first is cheaper by $.0025 per cup, × 24   Savings 6¢

I. The first is cheaper by $.0027888 per square foot, × 25

Savings 7¢

J. 3 25-foot hoses would cost $4.17, or $.0556 per foot. A 25- and a 50-foot hose would cost $3.75, or 5¢ per foot. A 30- and a 50-foot hose would cost $3.81, or $.047625 per foot. 3 30-foot

82 ◎ **Answers**

hoses would cost $4.35, or $.0483333 per foot. The second would cost the least in total price, but the third would cost the least per foot. The problem is ambiguous, but it would seem that the extra 5 feet would be appreciated, so let's buy the third. But since we don't want to cheat Mom, how do we figure the savings? Let's compare it with the fourth combination, instead of the first or second. The savings is $.0007083, × 80   Savings 6¢

K. The first is cheaper by $.0098215 per square inch, × 35   Savings 34¢

L. The second is cheaper by $.0148334 per exposure, × 36   Savings 53¢

The Calculator Murders

Most of the names can be read upside down on the calculator. Let us assign the proper number to each name:

Lise Bell—77383517   Bobo Hill—77140808
Hi Bishel—73451814   Elsie Lee—33731573
Max Carty—none   Eli Shill—77145173
Lil Ellis—51773717   Bob Sobel—73805808
Bill Hess—55347718   Ollie Sol—70531770

This list suggests that Max Carty is the culprit, and his motive is that his name cannot be read on a calculator, which makes him feel rejected and discriminated against. Since the first victim had the lowest number, and the second victim the next lowest number, it would seem that Bill Hess is the next person in line.

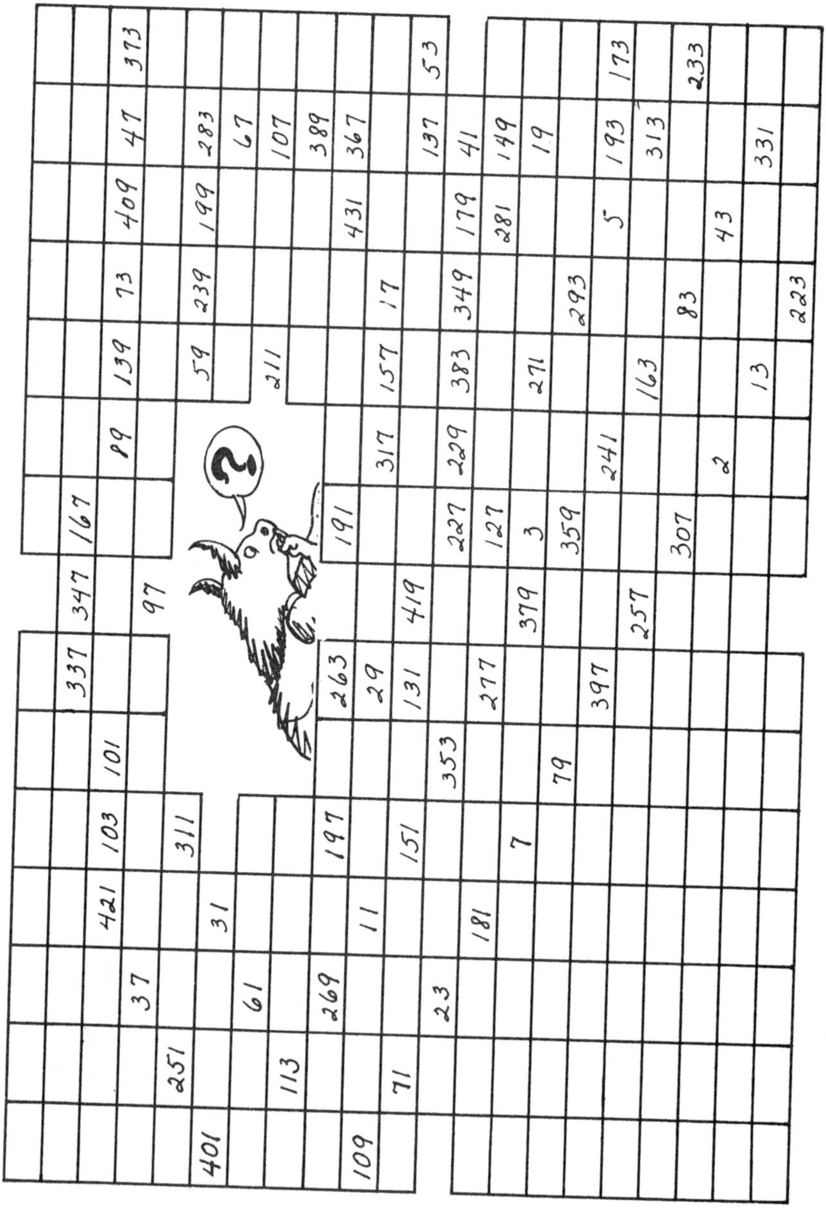

167 347 337
373 47 409 73 139 89 101 103 421
97 37
283 199 239 59 311 251
67 31 61 401
107 211 113
389 191 263 197 269
367 431 317 29 11 109
17 157 419 131 151 71
53 137
41 179 349 383 229 227 353 23
149 281 127 277 181
19 271 3 379 7
293 359 79
173 193 5 241 397
313 163 257
233 83 307
43 2
331 13
223

Minotaur

The diagram on page 84 shows the location of the prime numbers. You can easily chart the escape route through them.

Problems to Tax You

1. Dad's tax was figured as follows:

Income	13262.76	13263
Less 15%	1989.41	1989
Less 750 × 5	3750.00	3750
Net Income	7523.35	7524
Tax on 4,000	620.00	620
Tax on amount over 4,000 @ 19%	669.44	670
Total tax	1289.44	1290

The first calculation appears to be slightly off. But government regulations allow the accountant to round off the pennies on each entry made, and that is what he did, arriving at the second calculation.

2. The husband is entitled to $100. The wife is entitled to $18 plus half of $68, or $52 in all. Their combined deduction is $152.

3. Poor Mr. Sadde earned $100 this week, but his fixed deductions were $109.49, plus $39.85 on the percentage deductions, so that his take-home pay was −$49.34. Since he wants to double his take-home pay for next week, it should come to −$98.68. Next week his fixed deductions will come to $101.38, so he will have to earn the difference of $2.70 to cover his fixed deductions. This figure represents 60.15% of the total he will have to earn, $4.49 in all. His pay is $2.50 per hour, so he will have to work about 1.8 hours. Maybe he will use the extra time to look for a new job, or buy a ticket to the South Pole (on credit).

Timely Problems

1. Dad has 52 waking hours at home, so spends about 13.46% of his time on TV. Mom has 97 waking hours at home, so spends 21.65% of her time on TV and telephoning.

2. She will have to confine her television to about 6.06 hours a week, or about 6 hours 3½ minutes.

3. That all depends on how old you are. By multiplying 365 days per year times 24 hours per day times 60 minutes per hour times 60 seconds per minute, we learn that there are 31,536,000 seconds in a year. By dividing 1,000,000,000 by this figure (if it won't fit into your display, cross out the last three zeros of both dividend and divisor), we find that, if you have lived approximately 31.7 years, you've been around a billion seconds. These figures, of course, do not account for leap years, but why complicate matters?

4. This problem can best be approached by remembering the formula R × T = D, that is, rate of speed times time travelled equals distance covered. The car has travelled 250 miles at 150 m.p.h. This took up 1.6666666 hours, working to the accuracy of an eight-digit calculator. The total time it should take to travel 500 miles at 160 m.p.h. is 3.125 hours, meaning that the car must cover the remaining 250 miles in 1.4583334 hours, which requires a speed of 171.42856.

5. $600.

Problems of Interest

1. At 4%, put in 1 (dollar) and multiply by 1.04; continue to multiply by this constant until the display flips to 2. This would happen in the eighteenth year. At 5%, fifteenth year. At 6%, twelfth year. At 8%, tenth year. At 10%, eighth year.

2. Dad's monthly interest rate is .75%. His first month's interest comes to $75, leaving $225 to apply to the principal. In the second month his balance is $9,775, on which interest at .75% comes to $73.31, leaving $226.69 to apply to the principal. Notice that if you multiply $225 by 1.0075, you will get $226.69. Therefore, to find out how his payments on principal are increasing, you leave this figure (226.69) in your machine and keep multiplying by 1.0075, each multiplication (including the first month's payment of $225) representing 1 additional month's payment on the mortgage. But when should we stop, what figure are we trying to reach? Dad's monthly payment of $300—or almost. Suppose when we come down to the final month, his payment of $300 exactly covers the balance of the mortgage and the final month's interest. This would represent $297.77 on the mortgage (300 ÷ 1.0075) and $2.23 interest. Therefore, whenever the figure in your display shows less than $297.77, you will know that you have another month to go or more. If your display shows this figure or more, then you have completed the mortgage that month, possibly paying less than the full $300. At the end of the 38th month, he would have paid a total of $9,850.46 on his principal, leaving a balance due of $149.54 plus $1.12 interest to be paid in the 39th month.

3. It would be paid off in the 28th month. If you are eager for an even more difficult problem, you might imagine a situation where Dad sometimes paid $300 and sometimes $400.

4. Just a little. She bought merchandise worth $100, and was offered a 5% discount. Instead she bought merchandise worth $105 and received a $5 discount, or 4.76%. She should have received a 5% discount on the gift certificate, too.

5. You paid him 10% interest for a month. Some people would multiply this by 12, and say the interest rate was 120% for a year. A more accurate way to figure it is that at the end of

the first month he had $1.10 to invest, and could or did invest it at a rate of 10% per month, giving him $1.21 at the end of the second month. Carried through 12 months, he will end up with $3.14, or an annual interest rate of 214%.

6. Dad paid back $1,272, so his apparent interest rate is $\frac{72}{1200}$, or 6%. But he did not have the use of the $1,200 for a full year. His average balance was about half that, so his interest rate was about double, or 12%. You can figure out a more accurate rate on your calculator, if you are *interested*. Some people will say that the average amount of the loan was $650, interest $72, interest rate 11.0769%—but this does not take into consideration a compounding effect.

Home Improvements

1. There are 53.416666 square yards, but this equals only 90% of the material, which becomes 59.351851 square yards, or $445.14.

2. The ceiling equals 29.41176% of the total area, or $36.7647. $\frac{2}{3}$ of the price for the ceiling comes to $24.51 which ought to be saved, or a price of $100.49. Of course you can still argue that papering a ceiling is much harder than papering a wall, so he must have charged you proportionately more for the ceiling, and your savings should be greater.

3. $544.

4. If the dripping is driving you crazy, then by all means have it fixed, but, economically, you are far better off letting it drip. In the 8,760 hours in a standard year, the faucet will drip 438 gallons of water, which equals 101,178 cubic inches, which equals approximately 58.55 cubic feet. At the rate quoted in the problem, this much water costs only about 26¢ a year. Even if

the faucet dripped for 75 years, the cost of the water lost would not equal the plumber's fee.

5. $.34, approximately.

6. The first heater carries a total of $500 in warranties, which averages out to $50 for ten years. The second heater carries a total of $550 in warranties, or an average of $55. But when is the time of greatest danger? In the first year, when manufacturing defects usually show up, and in the latest years. Both heaters are equally protected in the first year, and the first heater not at all in the last five most dangerous years. The second heater would appear to be the better buy, unless you have some statistics to show that an unusually large proportion of these heaters go bad in the fifth year—the year when the advantage of the first heater over the second is the greatest.

Calculated Risk

No matter which of the four blocks you begin with, as you enter the system of tunnels the number in your machine will reach 12. After that, the numbers on all four direct routes are identical, so there is no point in seeking out a more desirable straight route.

You could go straight through to the center, but if you did, then all four axes would give you exactly the same answer, so that could hardly be the solution to the puzzle. But how can you get a lower score? Clearly, you must go through side tunnels which will decrease the number in the display of your calculator, rather than increase it.

There are three side tunnels in each level, but each can be travelled through in two directions, making six possibilities on each level. With a little experimentation, you will find the

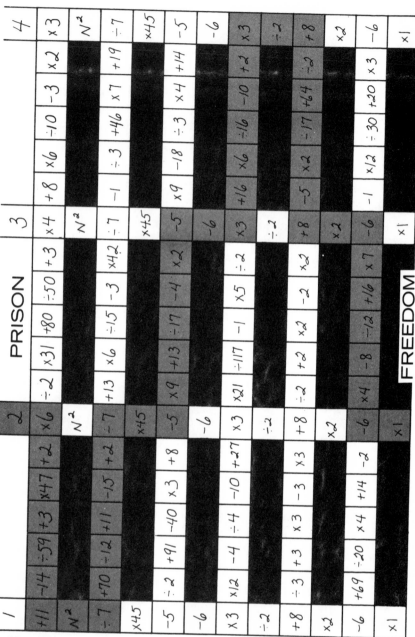

tunnel—and the direction—which will lower your score in the first level. Since all the other segments will increase your score, you may as well advance into the next level.

The maze could have been designed so that it might be necessary to go through a bad section in order to reach a desirable section, but that complication was not introduced in this puzzle. In any case, it is easily checked out. You know that you have reached the second level with the lowest possible figure. Test all the sections on the second level with that same starting figure, and you will find only one segment and direction on this level which lowers the score. You will always find, as the puzzle was designed, that the most desirable section and direction connects to the work you have already done, pointing the best way through the maze. See the diagram on page 90 for the best escape route.

Where There's a Will

1.

Wife	50%	.5 ÷ .97619	51.21953%
Son	33.3333%	.333333 ÷ .97619	34.14632%
Daughter	14.2857%	.142857 ÷ .97619	14.63413%
	97.619%		99.99998%
Dog	2.381%		
	100%		

2. $40,000 was the total amount of the estate. It is easy to figure that the wife got $37\frac{1}{2}$% and each son got $4\frac{1}{2}$% of the total, which, with the 25% to charity, means that the $11,400 which went to the daughter represented $28\frac{1}{2}$% of the total.

Oranges and Doughnuts

1. Perhaps you could set up the problem like this:

Number of Each Layer	Oranges in Layer	Total Oranges So Far	Is This a Square Number?
1	1	1	Yes, but not the answer
2	4	5	No
3	9	14	No
4	16	30	No
5	25	55	No

You can continue this table until the answer in the last column is yes. You can tell whether the answer is yes or no by taking the square root of the preceding number. If it comes out even the answer is yes. If your calculator does not have square root, you can estimate until you have two estimates, one below the number you are trying to reach, and one above it. Eventually you will hit it—at 4,900 in 24 layers.

2. To approach this problem, first find the area of the dough, then the area of the hole, and subtract to find the area of the piece of dough available. The area of each doughnut will be half this figure, but the area of the smaller doughnut must include the hole, and so the area of the hole (which we already figured in the second step) is added.

Now that we know the area of the smaller circle, all that remains is to go through the area formula (area $= \pi r^2$) backwards, that is, divide by π and then take the square root. This gives r, the radius, and twice this gives us the diameter of the inside doughnut.

The calculations are as follows:

Area of dough including hole	78.539815
Area of hole	.7853981
Area of dough without hole	77.754417

Area of each doughnut	38.877208
Area of smaller doughnut including hole	39.662606
$\div \pi$	12.624999
$\sqrt{}$	3.5531674
$\times 2$, gives diameter of small doughnut	7.1063348

Fuelish Figures

1. The cost per 100,000 B.T.U. is:

Gas	$.1562499
Coal	$.0833333
Fuel Oil	$.245614
Electricity	$1.1712

2. $.04896.
3. $6.
4. $5.0143.

Peasant Multiplication

If all of the halvings and doublings led you to suspect that the answer is found in the binary, or base 2, numbering system, you're on the right track. If you remember the first method shown on page 68 for transforming base 10 numbers to base 2, you will realize that by continually halving 39 in the first column, you have actually transformed it into its binary equivalent, 100111. The 1's in the binary number correspond to the odd numbers in the first column, the numbers which, in carrying over to the third column, you are actually multiplying by 71, as shown below.

1	0	0	1	1	1
					71
				142	
			284		
		568			
	1136				
2272					
2272			284	142	71

The value of 71 in the units column is 71. The value of 71 in the "tens" column is 142. The value of 71 in the "hundreds" column is 284. We carry below the line only those numbers whose value must be considered, and if that line is added across the answer will be 2769.

Car-ful Calculations

1.

Year	Repair	NEW CAR Cost	Av. Cost	USED CAR Cost	Av. Cost
1.	0	5000.00	5000.00		
2.	0	5000.00	2500.00		
3.	100.00	5100.00	1700.00	3100.00	3100.00
4.	150.00	5250.00	1312.50	3250.00	1625.00
5.	225.00	5475.00	1095.00	3475.00	1158.33
6.	337.50	5812.50	968.75	3812.50	953.13
7.	506.25	6318.75	902.68	4318.75	863.75
8.	759.38	7078.13	884.77	5078.13	846.36
9.	1139.06	8217.19	913.02	6217.19	888.17
10.	1708.59	9925.78	992.58	7925.78	990.72

It is no longer economical to keep a car when the cost of repairing it will cause the average annual cost to rise. On this basis, both cars become uneconomical after they are eight years old. The average cost of the used car, however, is lower over this period, and hence represents the better choice.

2. The trip across the border is going to cost you $1 for extra gasoline. To make up this dollar, at 5¢ profit per gallon, you would have to buy 20 gallons to break even, more to make a profit. But you are using up 2 gallons to make the trip, and want to return with a tankful of 20 extra gallons, so you would have to buy 22 gallons. It is assumed that the trip home would be made with the cheaper gasoline, and even though the trip out might be made with more expensive gasoline, the cheaper gasoline would replace it. But wait a minute. Was the choice between going across the border or staying home? The problem says the family enjoys riding. Maybe the choice was between going across the border or taking a 34-mile trip somewhere else, in which case you would not expect to return home with the same amount of gasoline, and so 20 becomes the correct answer.

Index

A CATALOG OF SELECTED
DOVER BOOKS
IN ALL FIELDS OF INTEREST

A CATALOG OF SELECTED
DOVER BOOKS
IN ALL FIELDS OF INTEREST

DRAWINGS OF REMBRANDT, edited by Seymour Slive. Updated Lippmann, Hofstede de Groot edition, with definitive scholarly apparatus. All portraits, biblical sketches, landscapes, nudes. Oriental figures, classical studies, together with selection of work by followers. 550 illustrations. Total of 630pp. 9⅛ × 12¼.
21485-0, 21486-9 Pa., Two-vol. set $29.90

GHOST AND HORROR STORIES OF AMBROSE BIERCE, Ambrose Bierce. 24 tales vividly imagined, strangely prophetic, and decades ahead of their time in technical skill: "The Damned Thing," "An Inhabitant of Carcosa," "The Eyes of the Panther," "Moxon's Master," and 20 more. 199pp. 5⅜ × 8½. 20767-6 Pa. $4.95

ETHICAL WRITINGS OF MAIMONIDES, Maimonides. Most significant ethical works of great medieval sage, newly translated for utmost precision, readability. Laws Concerning Character Traits, Eight Chapters, more. 192pp. 5⅜ × 8½.
24522-5 Pa. $5.95

THE EXPLORATION OF THE COLORADO RIVER AND ITS CANYONS, J. W. Powell. Full text of Powell's 1,000-mile expedition down the fabled Colorado in 1869. Superb account of terrain, geology, vegetation, Indians, famine, mutiny, treacherous rapids, mighty canyons, during exploration of last unknown part of continental U.S. 400pp. 5⅜ × 8½. 20094-9 Pa. $7.95

HISTORY OF PHILOSOPHY, Julián Marías. Clearest one-volume history on the market. Every major philosopher and dozens of others, to Existentialism and later. 505pp. 5⅜ × 8½. 21739-6 Pa. $9.95

ALL ABOUT LIGHTNING, Martin A. Uman. Highly readable nontechnical survey of nature and causes of lightning, thunderstorms, ball lightning, St. Elmo's Fire, much more. Illustrated. 192pp. 5⅜ × 8½. 25237-X Pa. $5.95

SAILING ALONE AROUND THE WORLD, Captain Joshua Slocum. First man to sail around the world, alone, in small boat. One of great feats of seamanship told in delightful manner. 67 illustrations. 294pp. 5⅜ × 8½. 20326-3 Pa. $4.95

LETTERS AND NOTES ON THE MANNERS, CUSTOMS AND CONDITIONS OF THE NORTH AMERICAN INDIANS, George Catlin. Classic account of life among Plains Indians: ceremonies, hunt, warfare, etc. 312 plates. 572pp. of text. 6⅛ × 9¼. 22118-0, 22119-9, Pa., Two-vol. set $17.90

THE SECRET LIFE OF SALVADOR DALÍ, Salvador Dalí. Outrageous but fascinating autobiography through Dalí's thirties with scores of drawings and sketches and 80 photographs. A must for lovers of 20th-century art. 432pp. 6½ × 9¼. (Available in U.S. only) 27454-3 Pa. $9.95

THE BOOK OF BEASTS: Being a Translation from a Latin Bestiary of the Twelfth Century, T. H. White. Wonderful catalog of real and fanciful beasts: manticore, griffin, phoenix, amphivius, jaculus, many more. White's witty erudite commentary on scientific, historical aspects enhances fascinating glimpse of medieval mind. Illustrated. 296pp. 5⅜ × 8¼. (Available in U.S. only)   24609-4 Pa. $7.95

FRANK LLOYD WRIGHT: Architecture and Nature with 160 Illustrations, Donald Hoffmann. Profusely illustrated study of influence of nature—especially prairie—on Wright's designs for Fallingwater, Robie House, Guggenheim Museum, other masterpieces. 96pp. 9¼ × 10¾.   25098-9 Pa. $8.95

FRANK LLOYD WRIGHT'S FALLINGWATER, Donald Hoffmann. Wright's famous waterfall house: planning and construction of organic idea. History of site, owners, Wright's personal involvement. Photographs of various stages of building. Preface by Edgar Kaufmann, Jr. 100 illustrations. 112pp. 9¼ × 10.
        23671-4 Pa. $8.95

YEARS WITH FRANK LLOYD WRIGHT: Apprentice to Genius, Edgar Tafel. Insightful memoir by a former apprentice presents a revealing portrait of Wright the man, the inspired teacher, the greatest American architect. 372 black-and-white illustrations. Preface. Index. vi + 228pp. 8¼ × 11.   24801-1 Pa. $10.95

THE STORY OF KING ARTHUR AND HIS KNIGHTS, Howard Pyle. Enchanting version of King Arthur fable has delighted generations with imaginative narratives of exciting adventures and unforgettable illustrations by the author. 41 illustrations. xviii + 313pp. 6⅛ × 9¼.   21445-1 Pa. $6.95

THE GODS OF THE EGYPTIANS, E. A. Wallis Budge. Thorough coverage of numerous gods of ancient Egypt by foremost Egyptologist. Information on evolution of cults, rites and gods; the cult of Osiris; the Book of the Dead and its rites; the sacred animals and birds; Heaven and Hell; and more. 956pp. 6⅛ × 9¼.
        22055-9, 22056-7 Pa., Two-vol. set $21.90

A THEOLOGICO-POLITICAL TREATISE, Benedict Spinoza. Also contains unfinished *Political Treatise*. Great classic on religious liberty, theory of government on common consent. R. Elwes translation. Total of 421pp. 5⅜ × 8½.
        20249-6 Pa. $7.95

INCIDENTS OF TRAVEL IN CENTRAL AMERICA, CHIAPAS, AND YUCATAN, John L. Stephens. Almost single-handed discovery of Maya culture; exploration of ruined cities, monuments, temples; customs of Indians. 115 drawings. 892pp. 5⅜ × 8½.   22404-X, 22405-8 Pa., Two-vol. set $17.90

LOS CAPRICHOS, Francisco Goya. 80 plates of wild, grotesque monsters and caricatures. Prado manuscript included. 183pp. 6⅞ × 9⅜.   22384-1 Pa. $6.95

AUTOBIOGRAPHY: The Story of My Experiments with Truth, Mohandas K. Gandhi. Not hagiography, but Gandhi in his own words. Boyhood, legal studies, purification, the growth of the Satyagraha (nonviolent protest) movement. Critical, inspiring work of the man who freed India. 480pp. 5⅜ × 8½. (Available in U.S. only)
        24593-4 Pa. $6.95

ILLUSTRATED DICTIONARY OF HISTORIC ARCHITECTURE, edited by Cyril M. Harris. Extraordinary compendium of clear, concise definitions for over 5,000 important architectural terms complemented by over 2,000 line drawings. Covers full spectrum of architecture from ancient ruins to 20th-century Modernism. Preface. 592pp. 7½ × 9⅝. 24444-X Pa. $15.95

THE NIGHT BEFORE CHRISTMAS, Clement Moore. Full text, and woodcuts from original 1848 book. Also critical, historical material. 19 illustrations. 40pp. 4⅝ × 6. 22797-9 Pa. $2.50

THE LESSON OF JAPANESE ARCHITECTURE: 165 Photographs, Jiro Harada. Memorable gallery of 165 photographs taken in the 1930's of exquisite Japanese homes of the well-to-do and historic buildings. 13 line diagrams. 192pp. 8⅜ × 11¼. 24778-3 Pa. $10.95

THE AUTOBIOGRAPHY OF CHARLES DARWIN AND SELECTED LETTERS, edited by Francis Darwin. The fascinating life of eccentric genius composed of an intimate memoir by Darwin (intended for his children); commentary by his son, Francis; hundreds of fragments from notebooks, journals, papers; and letters to and from Lyell, Hooker, Huxley, Wallace and Henslow. xi + 365pp. 5⅜ × 8. 20479-0 Pa. $6.95

WONDERS OF THE SKY: Observing Rainbows, Comets, Eclipses, the Stars and Other Phenomena, Fred Schaaf. Charming, easy-to-read poetic guide to all manner of celestial events visible to the naked eye. Mock suns, glories, Belt of Venus, more. Illustrated. 299pp. 5¼ × 8¼. 24402-4 Pa. $7.95

BURNHAM'S CELESTIAL HANDBOOK, Robert Burnham, Jr. Thorough guide to the stars beyond our solar system. Exhaustive treatment. Alphabetical by constellation: Andromeda to Cetus in Vol. 1; Chamaeleon to Orion in Vol. 2; and Pavo to Vulpecula in Vol. 3. Hundreds of illustrations. Index in Vol. 3. 2,000pp. 6⅛ × 9¼. 23567-X, 23568-8, 23673-0 Pa., Three-vol. set $41.85

STAR NAMES: Their Lore and Meaning, Richard Hinckley Allen. Fascinating history of names various cultures have given to constellations and literary and folkloristic uses that have been made of stars. Indexes to subjects. Arabic and Greek names. Biblical references. Bibliography. 563pp. 5⅜ × 8½. 21079-0 Pa. $8.95

THIRTY YEARS THAT SHOOK PHYSICS: The Story of Quantum Theory, George Gamow. Lucid, accessible introduction to influential theory of energy and matter. Careful explanations of Dirac's anti-particles, Bohr's model of the atom, much more. 12 plates. Numerous drawings. 240pp. 5⅜ × 8½. 24895-X Pa. $5.95

CHINESE DOMESTIC FURNITURE IN PHOTOGRAPHS AND MEASURED DRAWINGS, Gustav Ecke. A rare volume, now affordably priced for antique collectors, furniture buffs and art historians. Detailed review of styles ranging from early Shang to late Ming. Unabridged republication. 161 black-and-white drawings, photos. Total of 224pp. 8⅜ × 11¼. (Available in U.S. only) 25171-3 Pa. $13.95

VINCENT VAN GOGH: A Biography, Julius Meier-Graefe. Dynamic, penetrating study of artist's life, relationship with brother, Theo, painting techniques, travels, more. Readable, engrossing. 160pp. 5⅜ × 8½. (Available in U.S. only) 25253-1 Pa. $4.95

HOW TO WRITE, Gertrude Stein. Gertrude Stein claimed anyone could understand her unconventional writing—here are clues to help. Fascinating improvisations, language experiments, explanations illuminate Stein's craft and the art of writing. Total of 414pp. 4⅝ × 6⅜. 23144-5 Pa. $6.95

ADVENTURES AT SEA IN THE GREAT AGE OF SAIL: Five Firsthand Narratives, edited by Elliot Snow. Rare true accounts of exploration, whaling, shipwreck, fierce natives, trade, shipboard life, more. 33 illustrations. Introduction. 353pp. 5⅜ × 8½. 25177-2 Pa. $8.95

THE HERBAL OR GENERAL HISTORY OF PLANTS, John Gerard. Classic descriptions of about 2,850 plants—with over 2,700 illustrations—includes Latin and English names, physical descriptions, varieties, time and place of growth, more. 2,706 illustrations. xlv + 1,678pp. 8½ × 12¼. 23147-X Cloth. $75.00

DOROTHY AND THE WIZARD IN OZ, L. Frank Baum. Dorothy and the Wizard visit the center of the Earth, where people are vegetables, glass houses grow and Oz characters reappear. Classic sequel to *Wizard of Oz*. 256pp. 5⅜ × 8. 24714-7 Pa. $5.95

SONGS OF EXPERIENCE: Facsimile Reproduction with 26 Plates in Full Color, William Blake. This facsimile of Blake's original "Illuminated Book" reproduces 26 full-color plates from a rare 1826 edition. Includes "The Tyger," "London," "Holy Thursday," and other immortal poems. 26 color plates. Printed text of poems. 48pp. 5¼ × 7. 24636-1 Pa. $3.95

SONGS OF INNOCENCE, William Blake. The first and most popular of Blake's famous "Illuminated Books," in a facsimile edition reproducing all 31 brightly colored plates. Additional printed text of each poem. 64pp. 5¼ × 7. 22764-2 Pa. $3.95

PRECIOUS STONES, Max Bauer. Classic, thorough study of diamonds, rubies, emeralds, garnets, etc.: physical character, occurrence, properties, use, similar topics. 20 plates, 8 in color. 94 figures. 659pp. 6⅛ × 9¼. 21910-0, 21911-9 Pa., Two-vol. set $15.90

ENCYCLOPEDIA OF VICTORIAN NEEDLEWORK, S. F. A. Caulfeild and Blanche Saward. Full, precise descriptions of stitches, techniques for dozens of needlecrafts—most exhaustive reference of its kind. Over 800 figures. Total of 679pp. 8⅜ × 11. Two volumes. Vol. 1 22800-2 Pa. $11.95
Vol. 2 22801-0 Pa. $11.95

THE MARVELOUS LAND OF OZ, L. Frank Baum. Second Oz book, the Scarecrow and Tin Woodman are back with hero named Tip, Oz magic. 136 illustrations. 287pp. 5⅜ × 8½. 20692-0 Pa. $5.95

WILD FOWL DECOYS, Joel Barber. Basic book on the subject, by foremost authority and collector. Reveals history of decoy making and rigging, place in American culture, different kinds of decoys, how to make them, and how to use them. 140 plates. 156pp. 7⅞ × 10¾. 20011-6 Pa. $8.95

HISTORY OF LACE, Mrs. Bury Palliser. Definitive, profusely illustrated chronicle of lace from earliest times to late 19th century. Laces of Italy, Greece, England, France, Belgium, etc. Landmark of needlework scholarship. 266 illustrations. 672pp. 6⅛ × 9¼. 24742-2 Pa. $14.95

ILLUSTRATED GUIDE TO SHAKER FURNITURE, Robert Meader. All furniture and appurtenances, with much on unknown local styles. 235 photos. 146pp. 9 × 12. 22819-3 Pa. $8.95

WHALE SHIPS AND WHALING: A Pictorial Survey, George Francis Dow. Over 200 vintage engravings, drawings, photographs of barks, brigs, cutters, other vessels. Also harpoons, lances, whaling guns, many other artifacts. Comprehensive text by foremost authority. 207 black-and-white illustrations. 288pp. 6 × 9. 24808-9 Pa. $9.95

THE BERTRAMS, Anthony Trollope. Powerful portrayal of blind self-will and thwarted ambition includes one of Trollope's most heartrending love stories. 497pp. 5⅜ × 8½. 25119-5 Pa. $9.95

ADVENTURES WITH A HAND LENS, Richard Headstrom. Clearly written guide to observing and studying flowers and grasses, fish scales, moth and insect wings, egg cases, buds, feathers, seeds, leaf scars, moss, molds, ferns, common crystals, etc.—all with an ordinary, inexpensive magnifying glass. 209 exact line drawings aid in your discoveries. 220pp. 5⅜ × 8½. 23330-8 Pa. $4.95

RODIN ON ART AND ARTISTS, Auguste Rodin. Great sculptor's candid, wide-ranging comments on meaning of art; great artists; relation of sculpture to poetry, painting, music; philosophy of life, more. 76 superb black-and-white illustrations of Rodin's sculpture, drawings and prints. 119pp. 8⅜ × 11¼. 24487-3 Pa. $7.95

FIFTY CLASSIC FRENCH FILMS, 1912–1982: A Pictorial Record, Anthony Slide. Memorable stills from Grand Illusion, Beauty and the Beast, Hiroshima, Mon Amour, many more. Credits, plot synopses, reviews, etc. 160pp. 8¼ × 11. 25256-6 Pa. $11.95

THE PRINCIPLES OF PSYCHOLOGY, William James. Famous long course complete, unabridged. Stream of thought, time perception, memory, experimental methods; great work decades ahead of its time. 94 figures. 1,391pp. 5⅜ × 8½. 20381-6, 20382-4 Pa., Two-vol. set $23.90

BODIES IN A BOOKSHOP, R. T. Campbell. Challenging mystery of blackmail and murder with ingenious plot and superbly drawn characters. In the best tradition of British suspense fiction. 192pp. 5⅜ × 8½. 24720-1 Pa. $4.95

CALLAS: PORTRAIT OF A PRIMA DONNA, George Jellinek. Renowned commentator on the musical scene chronicles incredible career and life of the most controversial, fascinating, influential operatic personality of our time. 64 black-and-white photographs. 416pp. 5⅜ × 8¼. 25047-4 Pa. $8.95

GEOMETRY, RELATIVITY AND THE FOURTH DIMENSION, Rudolph Rucker. Exposition of fourth dimension, concepts of relativity as Flatland characters continue adventures. Popular, easily followed yet accurate, profound. 141 illustrations. 133pp. 5⅜ × 8½. 23400-2 Pa. $4.95

HOUSEHOLD STORIES BY THE BROTHERS GRIMM, with pictures by Walter Crane. 53 classic stories—Rumpelstiltskin, Rapunzel, Hansel and Gretel, the Fisherman and his Wife, Snow White, Tom Thumb, Sleeping Beauty, Cinderella, and so much more—lavishly illustrated with original 19th century drawings. 114 illustrations. x + 269pp. 5⅜ × 8½. 21080-4 Pa. $4.95

SUNDIALS, Albert Waugh. Far and away the best, most thorough coverage of ideas, mathematics concerned, types, construction, adjusting anywhere. Over 100 illustrations. 230pp. 5⅜ × 8½. 22947-5 Pa. $5.95

PICTURE HISTORY OF THE NORMANDIE: With 190 Illustrations, Frank O. Braynard. Full story of legendary French ocean liner: Art Deco interiors, design innovations, furnishings, celebrities, maiden voyage, tragic fire, much more. Extensive text. 144pp. 8⅜ × 11¾. 25257-4 Pa. $10.95

THE FIRST AMERICAN COOKBOOK: A Facsimile of "American Cookery," 1796, Amelia Simmons. Facsimile of the first American-written cookbook published in the United States contains authentic recipes for colonial favorites— pumpkin pudding, winter squash pudding, spruce beer, Indian slapjacks, and more. Introductory Essay and Glossary of colonial cooking terms. 80pp. 5⅜ × 8½. 24710-4 Pa. $3.50

101 PUZZLES IN THOUGHT AND LOGIC, C. R. Wylie, Jr. Solve murders and robberies, find out which fishermen are liars, how a blind man could possibly identify a color—purely by your own reasoning! 107pp. 5⅜ × 8½. 20367-0 Pa. $2.95

ANCIENT EGYPTIAN MYTHS AND LEGENDS, Lewis Spence. Examines animism, totemism, fetishism, creation myths, deities, alchemy, art and magic, other topics. Over 50 illustrations. 432pp. 5⅜ × 8½. 26525-0 Pa. $8.95

ANTHROPOLOGY AND MODERN LIFE, Franz Boas. Great anthropologist's classic treatise on race and culture. Introduction by Ruth Bunzel. Only inexpensive paperback edition. 255pp. 5⅜ × 8½. 25245-0 Pa. $7.95

THE TALE OF PETER RABBIT, Beatrix Potter. The inimitable Peter's terrifying adventure in Mr. McGregor's garden, with all 27 wonderful, full-color Potter illustrations. 55pp. 4¼ × 5½. (Available in U.S. only) 22827-4 Pa. $1.75

THREE PROPHETIC SCIENCE FICTION NOVELS, H. G. Wells. *When the Sleeper Wakes, A Story of the Days to Come* and *The Time Machine* (full version). 335pp. 5⅜ × 8½. (Available in U.S. only) 20605-X Pa. $8.95

APICIUS COOKERY AND DINING IN IMPERIAL ROME, edited and translated by Joseph Dommers Vehling. Oldest known cookbook in existence offers readers a clear picture of what foods Romans ate, how they prepared them, etc. 49 illustrations. 301pp. 6⅛ × 9¼. 23563-7 Pa. $7.95

SHAKESPEARE LEXICON AND QUOTATION DICTIONARY, Alexander Schmidt. Full definitions, locations, shades of meaning of every word in plays and poems. More than 50,000 exact quotations. 1,485pp. 6½ × 9¼. 22726-X, 22727-8 Pa., Two-vol. set $31.90

THE WORLD'S GREAT SPEECHES, edited by Lewis Copeland and Lawrence W. Lamm. Vast collection of 278 speeches from Greeks to 1970. Powerful and effective models; unique look at history. 842pp. 5⅜ × 8½. 20468-5 Pa. $12.95

CATALOG OF DOVER BOOKS

THE BLUE FAIRY BOOK, Andrew Lang. The first, most famous collection, with many familiar tales: Little Red Riding Hood, Aladdin and the Wonderful Lamp, Puss in Boots, Sleeping Beauty, Hansel and Gretel, Rumpelstiltskin; 37 in all. 138 illustrations. 390pp. 5⅜ × 8½. 21437-0 Pa. $6.95

THE STORY OF THE CHAMPIONS OF THE ROUND TABLE, Howard Pyle. Sir Launcelot, Sir Tristram and Sir Percival in spirited adventures of love and triumph retold in Pyle's inimitable style. 50 drawings, 31 full-page. xviii + 329pp. 6½ × 9¼. 21883-X Pa. $7.95

THE MYTHS OF THE NORTH AMERICAN INDIANS, Lewis Spence. Myths and legends of the Algonquins, Iroquois, Pawnees and Sioux with comprehensive historical and ethnological commentary. 36 illustrations. 5⅜ × 8½.
25967-6 Pa. $8.95

GREAT DINOSAUR HUNTERS AND THEIR DISCOVERIES, Edwin H. Colbert. Fascinating, lavishly illustrated chronicle of dinosaur research, 1820s to 1960. Achievements of Cope, Marsh, Brown, Buckland, Mantell, Huxley, many others. 384pp. 5¼ × 8¼. 24701-5 Pa. $7.95

THE TASTEMAKERS, Russell Lynes. Informal, illustrated social history of American taste 1850s-1950s. First popularized categories Highbrow, Lowbrow, Middlebrow. 129 illustrations. New (1979) afterword. 384pp. 6 × 9.
23993-4 Pa. $8.95

DOUBLE CROSS PURPOSES, Ronald A. Knox. A treasure hunt in the Scottish Highlands, an old map, unidentified corpse, surprise discoveries keep reader guessing in this cleverly intricate tale of financial skullduggery. 2 black-and-white maps. 320pp. 5⅜ × 8½. (Available in U.S. only) 25032-6 Pa. $6.95

AUTHENTIC VICTORIAN DECORATION AND ORNAMENTATION IN FULL COLOR: 46 Plates from "Studies in Design," Christopher Dresser. Superb full-color lithographs reproduced from rare original portfolio of a major Victorian designer. 48pp. 9¼ × 12¼. 25083-0 Pa. $7.95

PRIMITIVE ART, Franz Boas. Remains the best text ever prepared on subject, thoroughly discussing Indian, African, Asian, Australian, and, especially, Northern American primitive art. Over 950 illustrations show ceramics, masks, totem poles, weapons, textiles, paintings, much more. 376pp. 5⅜ × 8. 20025-6 Pa. $7.95

SIDELIGHTS ON RELATIVITY, Albert Einstein. Unabridged republication of two lectures delivered by the great physicist in 1920–21. *Ether and Relativity* and *Geometry and Experience.* Elegant ideas in nonmathematical form, accessible to intelligent layman. vi + 56pp. 5⅜ × 8½. 24511-X Pa. $3.95

THE WIT AND HUMOR OF OSCAR WILDE, edited by Alvin Redman. More than 1,000 ripostes, paradoxes, wisecracks: Work is the curse of the drinking classes, I can resist everything except temptation, etc. 258pp. 5⅜ × 8½. 20602-5 Pa. $4.95

ADVENTURES WITH A MICROSCOPE, Richard Headstrom. 59 adventures with clothing fibers, protozoa, ferns and lichens, roots and leaves, much more. 142 illustrations. 232pp. 5⅜ × 8½. 23471-1 Pa. $4.95

PLANTS OF THE BIBLE, Harold N. Moldenke and Alma L. Moldenke. Standard reference to all 230 plants mentioned in Scriptures. Latin name, biblical reference, uses, modern identity, much more. Unsurpassed encyclopedic resource for scholars, botanists, nature lovers, students of Bible. Bibliography. Indexes. 123 black-and-white illustrations. 384pp. 6 × 9. 25069-5 Pa. $8.95

FAMOUS AMERICAN WOMEN: A Biographical Dictionary from Colonial Times to the Present, Robert McHenry, ed. From Pocahontas to Rosa Parks, 1,035 distinguished American women documented in separate biographical entries. Accurate, up-to-date data, numerous categories, spans 400 years. Indices. 493pp. 6½ × 9¼. 24523-3 Pa. $10.95

THE FABULOUS INTERIORS OF THE GREAT OCEAN LINERS IN HISTORIC PHOTOGRAPHS, William H. Miller, Jr. Some 200 superb photographs capture exquisite interiors of world's great "floating palaces"—1890s to 1980s: *Titanic, Ile de France, Queen Elizabeth, United States, Europa,* more. Approx. 200 black-and-white photographs. Captions. Text. Introduction. 160pp. 8⅞ × 11¾. 24756-2 Pa. $9.95

THE GREAT LUXURY LINERS, 1927–1954: A Photographic Record, William H. Miller, Jr. Nostalgic tribute to heyday of ocean liners. 186 photos of *Ile de France, Normandie, Leviathan, Queen Elizabeth, United States,* many others. Interior and exterior views. Introduction. Captions. 160pp. 9 × 12. 24056-8 Pa. $12.95

A NATURAL HISTORY OF THE DUCKS, John Charles Phillips. Great landmark of ornithology offers complete detailed coverage of nearly 200 species and subspecies of ducks: gadwall, sheldrake, merganser, pintail, many more. 74 full-color plates, 102 black-and-white. Bibliography. Total of 1,920pp. 8⅝ × 11¼. 25141-1, 25142-X Cloth., Two-vol. set $100.00

THE SEAWEED HANDBOOK: An Illustrated Guide to Seaweeds from North Carolina to Canada, Thomas F. Lee. Concise reference covers 78 species. Scientific and common names, habitat, distribution, more. Finding keys for easy identification. 224pp. 5⅜ × 8½. 25215-9 Pa. $6.95

THE TEN BOOKS OF ARCHITECTURE: The 1755 Leoni Edition, Leon Battista Alberti. Rare classic helped introduce the glories of ancient architecture to the Renaissance. 68 black-and-white plates. 336pp. 8⅜ × 11¼. 25239-6 Pa. $14.95

MISS MACKENZIE, Anthony Trollope. Minor masterpieces by Victorian master unmasks many truths about life in 19th-century England. First inexpensive edition in years. 392pp. 5⅜ × 8½. 25201-9 Pa. $8.95

THE RIME OF THE ANCIENT MARINER, Gustave Doré, Samuel Taylor Coleridge. Dramatic engravings considered by many to be his greatest work. The terrifying space of the open sea, the storms and whirlpools of an unknown ocean, the ice of Antarctica, more—all rendered in a powerful, chilling manner. Full text. 38 plates. 77pp. 9¼ × 12. 22305-1 Pa. $4.95

THE EXPEDITIONS OF ZEBULON MONTGOMERY PIKE, Zebulon Montgomery Pike. Fascinating firsthand accounts (1805–6) of exploration of Mississippi River, Indian wars, capture by Spanish dragoons, much more. 1,088pp. 5⅜ × 8½. 25254-X, 25255-8 Pa., Two-vol. set $25.90

A CONCISE HISTORY OF PHOTOGRAPHY: Third Revised Edition, Helmut Gernsheim. Best one-volume history—camera obscura, photochemistry, daguerreotypes, evolution of cameras, film, more. Also artistic aspects—landscape, portraits, fine art, etc. 281 black-and-white photographs. 26 in color. 176pp. 8⅜ × 11¼.
25128-4 Pa. $14.95

THE DORÉ BIBLE ILLUSTRATIONS, Gustave Doré. 241 detailed plates from the Bible: the Creation scenes, Adam and Eve, Flood, Babylon, battle sequences, life of Jesus, etc. Each plate is accompanied by the verses from the King James version of the Bible. 241pp. 9 × 12.
23004-X Pa. $9.95

WANDERINGS IN WEST AFRICA, Richard F. Burton. Great Victorian scholar/adventurer's invaluable descriptions of African tribal rituals, fetishism, culture, art, much more. Fascinating 19th-century account. 624pp. 5⅜ × 8½. 26890-X Pa. $12.95

HISTORIC HOMES OF THE AMERICAN PRESIDENTS, Second Revised Edition, Irvin Haas. Guide to homes occupied by every president from Washington to Bush. Visiting hours, travel routes, more. 175 photos. 160pp. 8¼ × 11.
26751-2 Pa. $9.95

THE HISTORY OF THE LEWIS AND CLARK EXPEDITION, Meriwether Lewis and William Clark, edited by Elliott Coues. Classic edition of Lewis and Clark's day-by-day journals that later became the basis for U.S. claims to Oregon and the West. Accurate and invaluable geographical, botanical, biological, meteorological and anthropological material. Total of 1,508pp. 5⅜ × 8½.
21268-8, 21269-6, 21270-X Pa., Three-vol. set $29.85

LANGUAGE, TRUTH AND LOGIC, Alfred J. Ayer. Famous, clear introduction to Vienna, Cambridge schools of Logical Positivism. Role of philosophy, elimination of metaphysics, nature of analysis, etc. 160pp. 5⅜ × 8½. (Available in U.S. and Canada only)
20010-8 Pa. $3.95

MATHEMATICS FOR THE NONMATHEMATICIAN, Morris Kline. Detailed, college-level treatment of mathematics in cultural and historical context, with numerous exercises. For liberal arts students. Preface. Recommended Reading Lists. Tables. Index. Numerous black-and-white figures. xvi + 641pp. 5⅜ × 8½.
24823-2 Pa. $11.95

HANDBOOK OF PICTORIAL SYMBOLS, Rudolph Modley. 3,250 signs and symbols, many systems in full; official or heavy commercial use. Arranged by subject. Most in Pictorial Archive series. 143pp. 8¼ × 11. 23357-X Pa. $7.95

INCIDENTS OF TRAVEL IN YUCATAN, John L. Stephens. Classic (1843) exploration of jungles of Yucatan, looking for evidences of Maya civilization. Travel adventures, Mexican and Indian culture, etc. Total of 669pp. 5⅜ × 8½.
20926-1, 20927-X Pa., Two-vol. set $13.90

DEGAS: An Intimate Portrait, Ambroise Vollard. Charming, anecdotal memoir by famous art dealer of one of the greatest 19th-century French painters. 14 black-and-white illustrations. Introduction by Harold L. Van Doren. 96pp. 5⅜ × 8½.
25131-4 Pa. $4.95

PERSONAL NARRATIVE OF A PILGRIMAGE TO AL–MADINAH AND MECCAH, Richard F. Burton. Great travel classic by remarkably colorful personality. Burton, disguised as a Moroccan, visited sacred shrines of Islam, narrowly escaping death. 47 illustrations. 959pp. 5⅜ × 8½.
21217-3, 21218-1 Pa., Two-vol. set $19.90

PHRASE AND WORD ORIGINS, A. H. Holt. Entertaining, reliable, modern study of more than 1,200 colorful words, phrases, origins and histories. Much unexpected information. 254pp. 5⅜ × 8½.
20758-7 Pa. $5.95

THE RED THUMB MARK, R. Austin Freeman. In this first Dr. Thorndyke case, the great scientific detective draws fascinating conclusions from the nature of a single fingerprint. Exciting story, authentic science. 320pp. 5⅜ × 8½. (Available in U.S. only)
25210-8 Pa. $6.95

AN EGYPTIAN HIEROGLYPHIC DICTIONARY, E. A. Wallis Budge. Monumental work containing about 25,000 words or terms that occur in texts ranging from 3000 B.C. to 600 A.D. Each entry consists of a transliteration of the word, the word in hieroglyphs, and the meaning in English. 1,314pp. 6⅞ × 10.
23615-3, 23616-1 Pa., Two-vol. set $35.90

THE COMPLEAT STRATEGYST: Being a Primer on the Theory of Games of Strategy, J. D. Williams. Highly entertaining classic describes, with many illustrated examples, how to select best strategies in conflict situations. Prefaces. Appendices. xvi + 268pp. 5⅜ × 8½.
25101-2 Pa. $6.95

THE ROAD TO OZ, L. Frank Baum. Dorothy meets the Shaggy Man, little Button-Bright and the Rainbow's beautiful daughter in this delightful trip to the magical Land of Oz. 272pp. 5⅜ × 8.
25208-6 Pa. $5.95

POINT AND LINE TO PLANE, Wassily Kandinsky. Seminal exposition of role of point, line, other elements in nonobjective painting. Essential to understanding 20th-century art. 127 illustrations. 192pp. 6½ × 9¼.
23808-3 Pa. $5.95

LADY ANNA, Anthony Trollope. Moving chronicle of Countess Lovel's bitter struggle to win for herself and daughter Anna their rightful rank and fortune—perhaps at cost of sanity itself. 384pp. 5⅜ × 8½.
24669-8 Pa. $8.95

EGYPTIAN MAGIC, E. A. Wallis Budge. Sums up all that is known about magic in Ancient Egypt: the role of magic in controlling the gods, powerful amulets that warded off evil spirits, scarabs of immortality, use of wax images, formulas and spells, the secret name, much more. 253pp. 5⅜ × 8½.
22681-6 Pa. $4.95

THE DANCE OF SIVA, Ananda Coomaraswamy. Preeminent authority unfolds the vast metaphysic of India: the revelation of her art, conception of the universe, social organization, etc. 27 reproductions of art masterpieces. 192pp. 5⅜ × 8½.
24817-8 Pa. $6.95

CHRISTMAS CUSTOMS AND TRADITIONS, Clement A. Miles. Origin, evolution, significance of religious, secular practices. Caroling, gifts, yule logs, much more. Full, scholarly yet fascinating; non-sectarian. 400pp. 5⅜ × 8½.
23354-5 Pa. $7.95

THE HUMAN FIGURE IN MOTION, Eadweard Muybridge. More than 4,500 stopped-action photos, in action series, showing undraped men, women, children jumping, lying down, throwing, sitting, wrestling, carrying, etc. 390pp. 7⅞ × 10⅝.
20204-6 Cloth. $24.95

THE MAN WHO WAS THURSDAY, Gilbert Keith Chesterton. Witty, fast-paced novel about a club of anarchists in turn-of-the-century London. Brilliant social, religious, philosophical speculations. 128pp. 5⅜ × 8½.
25121-7 Pa. $3.95

A CÉZANNE SKETCHBOOK: Figures, Portraits, Landscapes and Still Lifes, Paul Cézanne. Great artist experiments with tonal effects, light, mass, other qualities in over 100 drawings. A revealing view of developing master painter, precursor of Cubism. 102 black-and-white illustrations. 144pp. 8¾ × 6⅜.
24790-2 Pa. $6.95

AN ENCYCLOPEDIA OF BATTLES: Accounts of Over 1,560 Battles from 1479 B.C. to the Present, David Eggenberger. Presents essential details of every major battle in recorded history, from the first battle of Megiddo in 1479 B.C. to Grenada in 1984. List of Battle Maps. New Appendix covering the years 1967–1984. Index. 99 illustrations. 544pp. 6½ × 9¼.
24913-1 Pa. $14.95

AN ETYMOLOGICAL DICTIONARY OF MODERN ENGLISH, Ernest Weekley. Richest, fullest work, by foremost British lexicographer. Detailed word histories. Inexhaustible. Total of 856pp. 6½ × 9¼.
21873-2, 21874-0 Pa., Two-vol. set $19.90

WEBSTER'S AMERICAN MILITARY BIOGRAPHIES, edited by Robert McHenry. Over 1,000 figures who shaped 3 centuries of American military history. Detailed biographies of Nathan Hale, Douglas MacArthur, Mary Hallaren, others. Chronologies of engagements, more. Introduction. Addenda. 1,033 entries in alphabetical order. xi + 548pp. 6½ × 9¼. (Available in U.S. only)
24758-9 Pa. $13.95

LIFE IN ANCIENT EGYPT, Adolf Erman. Detailed older account, with much not in more recent books: domestic life, religion, magic, medicine, commerce, and whatever else needed for complete picture. Many illustrations. 597pp. 5⅜ × 8½.
22632-8 Pa. $9.95

HISTORIC COSTUME IN PICTURES, Braun & Schneider. Over 1,450 costumed figures shown, covering a wide variety of peoples: kings, emperors, nobles, priests, servants, soldiers, scholars, townsfolk, peasants, merchants, courtiers, cavaliers, and more. 256pp. 8⅜ × 11¼.
23150-X Pa. $9.95

THE NOTEBOOKS OF LEONARDO DA VINCI, edited by J. P. Richter. Extracts from manuscripts reveal great genius; on painting, sculpture, anatomy, sciences, geography, etc. Both Italian and English. 186 ms. pages reproduced, plus 500 additional drawings, including studies for *Last Supper*, *Sforza* monument, etc. 860pp. 7⅞ × 10¾. (Available in U.S. only) 22572-0, 22573-9 Pa., Two-vol. set $35.90

THE ART NOUVEAU STYLE BOOK OF ALPHONSE MUCHA: All 72 Plates from "Documents Decoratifs" in Original Color, Alphonse Mucha. Rare copyright-free design portfolio by high priest of Art Nouveau. Jewelry, wallpaper, stained glass, furniture, figure studies, plant and animal motifs, etc. Only complete one-volume edition. 80pp. 9⅜ × 12¼. 24044-4 Pa. $9.95

ANIMALS: 1,419 COPYRIGHT-FREE ILLUSTRATIONS OF MAMMALS, BIRDS, FISH, INSECTS, ETC., edited by Jim Harter. Clear wood engravings present, in extremely lifelike poses, over 1,000 species of animals. One of the most extensive pictorial sourcebooks of its kind. Captions. Index. 284pp. 9 × 12. 23766-4 Pa. $9.95

OBELISTS FLY HIGH, C. Daly King. Masterpiece of American detective fiction, long out of print, involves murder on a 1935 transcontinental flight—"a very thrilling story"—NY Times. Unabridged and unaltered republication of the edition published by William Collins Sons & Co. Ltd., London, 1935. 288pp. 5⅜ × 8½. (Available in U.S. only) 25036-9 Pa. $5.95

VICTORIAN AND EDWARDIAN FASHION: A Photographic Survey, Alison Gernsheim. First fashion history completely illustrated by contemporary photographs. Full text plus 235 photos, 1840–1914, in which many celebrities appear. 240pp. 6½ × 9¼. 24205-6 Pa. $8.95

THE ART OF THE FRENCH ILLUSTRATED BOOK, 1700–1914, Gordon N. Ray. Over 630 superb book illustrations by Fragonard, Delacroix, Daumier, Doré, Grandville, Manet, Mucha, Steinlen, Toulouse-Lautrec and many others. Preface. Introduction. 633 halftones. Indices of artists, authors & titles, binders and provenances. Appendices. Bibliography. 608pp. 8⅜ × 11¼. 25086-5 Pa. $24.95

THE WONDERFUL WIZARD OF OZ, L. Frank Baum. Facsimile in full color of America's finest children's classic. 143 illustrations by W. W. Denslow. 267pp. 5⅜ × 8½. 20691-2 Pa. $7.95

FOLLOWING THE EQUATOR: A Journey Around the World, Mark Twain. Great writer's 1897 account of circumnavigating the globe by steamship. Ironic humor, keen observations, vivid and fascinating descriptions of exotic places. 197 illustrations. 720pp. 5⅜ × 8½. 26113-1 Pa. $15.95

THE FRIENDLY STARS, Martha Evans Martin & Donald Howard Menzel. Classic text marshalls the stars together in an engaging, non-technical survey, presenting them as sources of beauty in night sky. 23 illustrations. Foreword. 2 star charts. Index. 147pp. 5⅜ × 8½. 21099-5 Pa. $3.95

FADS AND FALLACIES IN THE NAME OF SCIENCE, Martin Gardner. Fair, witty appraisal of cranks, quacks, and quackeries of science and pseudoscience: hollow earth, Velikovsky, orgone energy, Dianetics, flying saucers, Bridey Murphy, food and medical fads, etc. Revised, expanded In the Name of Science. "A very able and even-tempered presentation."—The New Yorker. 363pp. 5⅜ × 8. 20394-8 Pa. $6.95

ANCIENT EGYPT: ITS CULTURE AND HISTORY, J. E Manchip White. From pre-dynastics through Ptolemies: society, history, political structure, religion, daily life, literature, cultural heritage. 48 plates. 217pp. 5⅜ × 8½. 22548-8 Pa. $5.95

CATALOG OF DOVER BOOKS

SIR HARRY HOTSPUR OF HUMBLETHWAITE, Anthony Trollope. Incisive, unconventional psychological study of a conflict between a wealthy baronet, his idealistic daughter, and their scapegrace cousin. The 1870 novel in its first inexpensive edition in years. 250pp. 5⅜ × 8½. 24953-0 Pa. $6.95

LASERS AND HOLOGRAPHY, Winston E. Kock. Sound introduction to burgeoning field, expanded (1981) for second edition. Wave patterns, coherence, lasers, diffraction, zone plates, properties of holograms, recent advances. 84 illustrations. 160pp. 5⅜ × 8¼. (Except in United Kingdom) 24041-X Pa. $3.95

INTRODUCTION TO ARTIFICIAL INTELLIGENCE: Second, Enlarged Edition, Philip C. Jackson, Jr. Comprehensive survey of artificial intelligence—the study of how machines (computers) can be made to act intelligently. Includes introductory and advanced material. Extensive notes updating the main text. 132 black-and-white illustrations. 512pp. 5⅜ × 8½. 24864-X Pa. $10.95

HISTORY OF INDIAN AND INDONESIAN ART, Ananda K. Coomaraswamy. Over 400 illustrations illuminate classic study of Indian art from earliest Harappa finds to early 20th century. Provides philosophical, religious and social insights. 304pp. 6⅜ × 9⅜. 25005-9 Pa. $11.95

THE GOLEM, Gustav Meyrink. Most famous supernatural novel in modern European literature, set in Ghetto of Old Prague around 1890. Compelling story of mystical experiences, strange transformations, profound terror. 13 black-and-white illustrations. 224pp. 5⅜ × 8½. (Available in U.S. only) 25025-3 Pa. $6.95

PICTORIAL ENCYCLOPEDIA OF HISTORIC ARCHITECTURAL PLANS, DETAILS AND ELEMENTS: With 1,880 Line Drawings of Arches, Domes, Doorways, Facades, Gables, Windows, etc., John Theodore Haneman. Sourcebook of inspiration for architects, designers, others. Bibliography. Captions. 141pp. 9 × 12. 24605-1 Pa. $8.95

BENCHLEY LOST AND FOUND, Robert Benchley. Finest humor from early 30s, about pet peeves, child psychologists, post office and others. Mostly unavailable elsewhere. 73 illustrations by Peter Arno and others. 183pp. 5⅜ × 8½. 22410-4 Pa. $4.95

ERTÉ GRAPHICS, Erté. Collection of striking color graphics: Seasons, Alphabet, Numerals, Aces and Precious Stones. 50 plates, including 4 on covers. 48pp. 9⅜ × 12¼. 23580-7 Pa. $7.95

THE JOURNAL OF HENRY D. THOREAU, edited by Bradford Torrey, F. H. Allen. Complete reprinting of 14 volumes, 1837–61, over two million words; the sourcebooks for Walden, etc. Definitive. All original sketches, plus 75 photographs. 1,804pp. 8½ × 12¼. 20312-3, 20313-1 Cloth., Two-vol. set $130.00

CASTLES: Their Construction and History, Sidney Toy. Traces castle development from ancient roots. Nearly 200 photographs and drawings illustrate moats, keeps, baileys, many other features. Caernarvon, Dover Castles, Hadrian's Wall, Tower of London, dozens more. 256pp. 5⅜ × 8¼. 24898-4 Pa. $7.95

AMERICAN CLIPPER SHIPS: 1833–1858, Octavius T. Howe & Frederick C. Matthews. Fully-illustrated, encyclopedic review of 352 clipper ships from the period of America's greatest maritime supremacy. Introduction. 109 halftones. 5 black-and-white line illustrations. Index. Total of 928pp. 5⅜ × 8½.
25115-2, 25116-0 Pa., Two-vol. set $17.90

TOWARDS A NEW ARCHITECTURE, Le Corbusier. Pioneering manifesto by great architect, near legendary founder of "International School." Technical and aesthetic theories, views on industry, economics, relation of form to function, "mass-production spirit," much more. Profusely illustrated. Unabridged translation of 13th French edition. Introduction by Frederick Etchells. 320pp. 6⅛ × 9¼. (Available in U.S. only)
25023-7 Pa. $8.95

THE BOOK OF KELLS, edited by Blanche Cirker. Inexpensive collection of 32 full-color, full-page plates from the greatest illuminated manuscript of the Middle Ages, painstakingly reproduced from rare facsimile edition. Publisher's Note. Captions. 32pp. 9⅜ × 12¼. (Available in U.S. only)
24345-1 Pa. $5.95

BEST SCIENCE FICTION STORIES OF H. G. WELLS, H. G. Wells. Full novel *The Invisible Man*, plus 17 short stories: "The Crystal Egg," "Aepyornis Island," "The Strange Orchid," etc. 303pp. 5⅜ × 8½. (Available in U.S. only)
21531-8 Pa. $6.95

AMERICAN SAILING SHIPS: Their Plans and History, Charles G. Davis. Photos, construction details of schooners, frigates, clippers, other sailcraft of 18th to early 20th centuries—plus entertaining discourse on design, rigging, nautical lore, much more. 137 black-and-white illustrations. 240pp. 6⅛ × 9¼.
24658-2 Pa. $6.95

ENTERTAINING MATHEMATICAL PUZZLES, Martin Gardner. Selection of author's favorite conundrums involving arithmetic, money, speed, etc., with lively commentary. Complete solutions. 112pp. 5⅜ × 8½.
25211-6 Pa. $3.50

THE WILL TO BELIEVE, HUMAN IMMORTALITY, William James. Two books bound together. Effect of irrational on logical, and arguments for human immortality. 402pp. 5⅜ × 8½.
20291-7 Pa. $8.95

THE HAUNTED MONASTERY and THE CHINESE MAZE MURDERS, Robert Van Gulik. 2 full novels by Van Gulik continue adventures of Judge Dee and his companions. An evil Taoist monastery, seemingly supernatural events; overgrown topiary maze that hides strange crimes. Set in 7th-century China. 27 illustrations. 328pp. 5⅜ × 8½.
23502-5 Pa. $6.95

CELEBRATED CASES OF JUDGE DEE (DEE GOONG AN), translated by Robert Van Gulik. Authentic 18th-century Chinese detective novel; Dee and associates solve three interlocked cases. Led to Van Gulik's own stories with same characters. Extensive introduction. 9 illustrations. 237pp. 5⅜ × 8½.
23337-5 Pa. $5.95

Prices subject to change without notice.

Available at your book dealer or write for free catalog to Dept. GI, Dover Publications, Inc., 31 East 2nd St., Mineola, N.Y. 11501. Dover publishes more than 175 books each year on science, elementary and advanced mathematics, biology, music, art, literary history, social sciences and other areas.